STUDY GUID
for

D0361658

The Enjoyment
of Music

Ninth Edition

The Enjoyment of Music

NINTH EDITION

Kristine Forney

CALIFORNIA STATE UNIVERSITY, LONG BEACH

 W • W • NORTON & COMPANY • NEW YORK • LONDON

ISBN: 0-393-97980-6 (pbk.)

W. W. Norton & Company, Inc., 500 Fifth Avenue, New York, N.Y. 10110
www.wwnorton.com
W. W. Norton & Company Ltd., Castle House, 75/76 Wells Street, London W1T 3QT

2 3 4 5 6 7 8 9 0

Contents

Preface

This Study Guide, which accompanies *The Enjoyment of Music*, Ninth Edition, is designed to help you get the most out of your music studies by reinforcing the information in the text and by guiding you in the exploration of new musical styles. This workbook is organized to coincide with the Chronological and Shorter versions of the text; it is, of course, also designed for use with the Standard version. Exercises throughout the guide are keyed to chapters, Listening Guides (LG), and Cultural Perspectives (CP) in all versions of the text. In this Guide you will find the following:

- Forty-three *Review* exercises, based on the most important terms, concepts, and historical information in the text. These exercises test your knowledge and understanding through objective questions (multiple choice, true or false, matching, and short answer). For some questions, you are asked to consider an idea and give your opinion. These questions are designed to help you prepare for exams and quizzes. Your instructor may assign review exercises to be completed and turned in (you will notice that the pages are perforated for easy removal) or may suggest that you do them on your own to reinforce your studying. Web-based reviews for elements of music exercises 2–6 and era transitions are signaled here with a computer icon and may be found at www.wwnorton.com/enjoy.

- Forty-two *Listen* exercises that help guide your study of the musical selections outlined in the text (in Listening Guides) and included on the recording set. Note that each question about works that are included only on the larger 8-CD set of *The Norton Recordings* (which accompanies the Chronological and Standard versions) has an asterisk (*) next to it; if you are using the Shorter text and the 4-CD set of recordings, you should skip the asterisked items. The questions ask you to describe certain musical elements you hear, and also to review the history and form of each work. Before completing these listening exercises, you should read about the work and listen to it while following the Listening Guide in the text or the electronic Listening Guides (eLGs) on your enhanced CDs.

- Twenty-three *Explore* studies that review your understanding of the information presented in the Cultural Perspectives throughout the text. These guides are designed to broaden your knowledge of traditional, popular, and certain non-Western musics by opening windows on these cultures to see how they have influenced Western art music or been influenced by it. For each of these exercises, there is an outside assignment suggested (listening or Web-based) that allows you some freedom to explore another style of music and write about it. These exercises may be assigned by the instructor as either required or extra-credit work, or you may be left to decide which you are most interested in doing outside of class. A computer icon signals the Web assignment at www.wwnorton.com/enjoy; once there click on Cultural Perspectives.

- Fifteen *Music Activities* that allow you more direct and sometimes "hands-on" experience with music. These may be assigned to you to do alone, in some cases on the Web, or in small groups (study groups or discussion sections). The introduction to this section on page 217 provides more information about these guides.

- Five *Concert Report* outlines for completion during or after concerts. Since most music appreciation classes require concert attendance and written reports, these forms may be completed and turned in or may serve as outlines for prose reports, depending on course requirements. The introduction to this section on page 249 lists the different outlines provided and the types of music for which each should be used. Included are a sample completed outline based on a hypothetical concert and a sample prose report.

Note, too, that we have provided an *Online Tutor* as an alternate (or additional) means of reviewing terms and listening assignments, and exploring the Cultural Perspectives from the text. You may access this tutor at www.wwnorton.com/enjoy.

This Study Guide also includes two surveys: one to complete at the beginning of the course and one to fill out at its close. Instructors may wish to collect these surveys to familiarize themselves with the musical tastes and experiences of their students, or you may use them to gauge how your own tastes and experiences have changed as a result of taking the class, reading *The Enjoyment of Music* text, and using the accompanying materials.

I wish to express my sincere appreciation to the many faculty who have offered helpful suggestions for this edition of the guide, to my colleagues at California State University, Long Beach, for their contributions and unflagging loyalty, and to the many students on whom I have tried out these exercises. Through the use of these materials, they arrived, as I hope you will, at a new "enjoyment of music." I am much indebted to Michael Ochs, former music editor at W. W. Norton, for his good-natured guidance and expert copyediting of this study guide.

Kristine Forney

Note on Abbreviations

Throughout this Study Guide, the following abbreviations are used:

Chr = Chronological version of *The Enjoyment of Music,* 9th ed.
Sh   = Shorter version of the text
Std = Standard version of the text
LG = Listening Guide
CP = Cultural Perspective
*e***LG** = Electronic Listening Guide on enhanced CD set
♪   = eMusic, on Resource CD
🎵 = Resource CD
[e] = www.wwnorton.com/enjoy

References to the three different versions of the book are given by chapter number; use the Table of Contents in the textbook to locate the page number for each chapter. References to Listening Guides are given by LG numbers and to Cultural Perspectives by CP numbers. For quick access to these pages in the text, consult the Tables of Cultural Perspectives and Listening Guides in the front of your textbook. A Table of Listening Guides and Recordings is printed inside the cover of your textbook to help you locate the musical selections on whichever recording package you are using.

Pre-Course Survey

Level: ___ Freshman ___ Sophomore ___ Junior ___ Senior ___ Grad

___ High school ___ Adult education Other _____

General Information

Major (or undeclared): _____

Minor area (or undeclared): _____

Why did you choose to take this course?

___ general education credit ___ free elective ___ enjoy music

___ required for major ___ convenient time ___ instructor

How did you hear about this course?

___ recommended by adviser ___ recommended by student(s)

___ found on my own ___ other _____

Musical Tastes

How often do you listen to music? ___ frequently ___ sometimes

___ infrequently ___ never

What music listening equipment do you have available?

___ radio ___ cassette ___ CD player ___ CD-ROM drive

___ MP3 player ___ car stereo ___ DAT player other _____

What styles of music do you prefer to listen to? _____

_____

Name two favorite compositions (in any style).

_____

_____

List two favorite performers or performing groups.

_____

_____

Do you attend live concerts? ___ often ___ occasionally ___ rarely ___ never

If yes, name one you particularly enjoyed.

_____

Musical Background

Check the musical experiences that apply.

___ Played an instrument   Which instrument? _____

___ Took music lessons   How many years? _____

___ Played or sang in a group

    ___ concert band   ___ orchestra   ___ chorus   ___ rock band

    ___ Broadway musical   ___ jazz ensemble   ___ church choir

    other _____

___ Studied music theory or music appreciation

Which of the following types of concerts have you attended? Name the group or a work performed, if you remember.

___ orchestra _____

___ opera _____

___ musical _____

___ ballet _____

___ concert band _____

___ jazz band _____

___ rock band _____

___ choir/chorus _____

___ solo recital _____

___ chamber group _____

___ world music _____

___ folk music _____

___ other _____

What do you hope to learn in this course? _____

_____

_____

_____

1. *Explore* Music and Today's Listener: The State of the Art
CP 1 Chr/Sh/Std

Exercises

1. Compare some traditional ways of listening to music with more recent, technologically-enhanced ways.

TRADITIONAL TECHNOLOGIES   RECENT TECHNOLOGIES

_____   _____

_____   _____

_____   _____

_____   _____

2. What are some advantages of listening to Internet radio?

_____

_____

_____

3. What are some advantages of listening to (or watching) a Webcast of a concert?

_____

_____

_____

4. What are some advantages of the MP3 format? What controversy surrounds it?

_____

_____

_____

_____

_____

5. How have these new technologies affected performers, composers, and songwriters?

_____

_____

_____

_____

1

Essay

Write an essay that includes consideration of the following questions:

1. What do you think the future holds for music online?
2. How should we resolve the file-sharing controversy?
3. Will a new business model present itself that satisfies consumers and artists alike?

_____

_____

_____

_____

_____

_____

_____

_____

_____

_____

_____

_____

_____

_____

_____

_____

_____

_____

_____

_____

_____

_____

_____

_____

_____

---

2. *Review* Elements of Music: Melody and Rhythm
Chaps. 1–2 Chr/Sh/Std

Terms to Remember

musical sound	type of movement	measure	compound meter
pitch	conjunct	beat	sextuple
frequency	disjunct	unaccented	additive meter
duration	structure of melody	accented	upbeat
melody	phrase	simple meter	syncopation
interval	cadence	duple	polyrhythm
range	countermelody	triple	nonmetric
shape	rhythm	quadruple	
	meter		

Exercises

Complete the following questions.

1. A musical sound (tone) can be defined in terms of its _____ and its _____.

2. _____ is the number of vibrations per second.

3. The distance between two different pitches is a(n) _____.

4. A(n) _____ is a coherent succession of pitches, heard as a unity.

5. A melody that moves by small intervals in a connected style is called _____, while one with many leaps is called _____.

6. The characteristic of melody that describes its direction or movement up and down is referred to as its _____ while the distance between its highest and lowest notes is its _____.

7. A resting point in a melody is known as a(n)_____.

8. The melody of *Amazing Grace* ♪ (on p. 16 of the text) is organized into four equal parts known as _____.

9. The regular pulse and basic unit of length heard in most Western music is called the _____.

10. Those pulses that are stronger than others are known as _____, while weaker pulses are called _____.

11. The organizing factor in music that sets fixed time patterns is called _____.

12. Meters that subdivide beats into groups of two are called_____.

13. Meters that subdivide beats into groups of three are called _____.

14. The meter of the patriotic song *America the Beautiful* is best described as _____. Rather than beginning on the downbeat or first beat, it begins with a(n) _____.

15. The most likely meter for a march would be _____.

16. The rhythmic procedure that is used to temporarily upset or throw off the meter is called _____.

17. The simultaneous use of two or more rhythmic patterns is called _____, and is heard in (styles) _____.

18. Groupings of irregular numbers of beats that add up to an overall larger pattern produces a(n) _____ meter.

19. Music with a weak or veiled beat may be considered _____.

Sing through or listen to the entire melody of *America (My Country, 'Tis of Thee)* ♪ (p. 35 of the text) before answering the questions 20–22. Check the correct answer for each.

20. Is this melody principally: ___ conjunct (connected, smooth) or
                                 ___ disjunct (disjointed, with leaps)?

21. Is the range of this melody: ___ narrow (spanning few notes) or
                                 ___ wide (spanning many notes)?

22. Is the shape of the melody: ___ wavelike or
                                ___ a straight line?

Consider the rhythm and meter of the well-known song *Happy Birthday* before answering questions 23–25.

Text:	Hap-py	birth-	day	to	you_____,
Meter:	3	1	2	3	1	2

Text:	Hap-py	birth-	day	to	you_____,
Meter:	3	1	2	3	1	2

23. What meter is indicated in the example? ___ duple   ___ triple
                                            ___ quadruple ___ sextuple

24. On which beat does the song begin? _____

25. This is an example of ___ simple meter or ___ compound meter

3. *Review* Elements of Music: Harmony and Texture
Chaps. 3–4 Chr/Sh/Std

Terms to Remember

harmony	dissonance	texture	canon
chord	consonance	monophonic	round
scale	scale	heterophonic	inversion
octave	major	polyphonic	retrograde
triad	minor	homophonic	retrograde
tonic	diatonic	homorhythmic	inversion
tonality	chromatic	counterpoint	augmentation
syllables	drone	imitation	diminution

Exercises

Complete the following questions.

1. The element of music that pertains to the movement and relationship of intervals and chords is _____.

2. What are the syllables used to identify the tones of the scale?

    _do_ ____ ____ ____ ____ ____ ____ ____

3. An octave is the interval from *do* to _____ in the scale.

4. The interval of a fifth in syllables is *do* to _____.

5. Three or more tones sounded together are called a(n) _____.

6. A triad is a three-note chord built from alternate scale tones, such as

    _do_ ____ ____. In numbers, it would be scale tones _1_ ___ ___.

7. In the organizing system known as tonality, the first scale tone or

    keynote is known as the _____.

8. The two scale types that are commonly found in Western music from

    around 1650 to 1900 are _____ and _____.

9. Music built from the tones of one of the scale types above is referred to

    as _____ while music built from the full range of notes

    in the octave is referred to as _____.

10. On which scale would a lament probably be built? _____

11. Unstable musical sounds in need of resolution are called

    _____.

    How might they sound?_____

12. Musical sounds that seem stable, not needing to resolve, are called

    _____.

    How might they sound?_____

13. Some musics unfold over a supporting sustained tone, or

    _____.

14. The element of music that refers to its fabric or the interplay of its

    parts is known as _____.

15. Music with a single melodic line and no accompaniment is called

    _____ texture, whereas a musical texture with a single

    melody and a chordal accompaniment is called _____.

16. A texture in which all voices move together with the same rhythm in a

    note-against-note style is called _____.

17. _____ is a texture that combines two or more melodic voices.

18. A melody combined with an ornamented version of itself produces a

    texture known as _____. In what styles of music does

    this frequently occur? _____

19. The art of combining two or more voices into a single texture is known

    as _____. Its name means "note against note."

20. Overlapping statements of the same melody in several parts is known as

    _____, producing a _____ texture.

21. A strictly ordered composition based on one voice imitating another is

    called a _____, or more popularly, a _____.

22. When a melody is heard backward, it is in _____.

23. When a melody is turned upside down, so that its intervals occur in the

    opposite direction, the technique is called _____.

24. _____ means a melody is heard more slowly (half as

    fast).

25. The opposite technique, in which a melody is presented faster than its

    original form, is called _____.

26. Which texture would be heard if *Happy Birthday* were sung with no

    accompaniment? _____

    With piano accompaniment? _____

4. *Review* Elements of Music: Form
Chap. 5 Chr/Sh/Std

Terms to Remember

form	binary form	thematic development
repetition	ternary form	call and response
contrast	theme	ostinato
variation	motive	movement
improvisation	sequence	

Exercises

Complete the following questions.

1. The element of music representing clarity and order is _____.

2. The two basic principles of musical structure are _____ and _____. A third principle of form is _____.

3. Binary form can best be outlined as _____. Which principle of form (from question 2) is central to this scheme? _____

4. Ternary form can best be outlined as _____. Which principles of form does this structure illustrate? _____

5. Pieces created by performers during the performance (as opposed to being precomposed) are based on _____. In which styles of music is this technique common? _____

6. A _____ is a melody used as a building block in a work. This melody can be broken up into smaller units, or _____, and it can be restated at another pitch level, or in _____.

7. Expansion of a theme is called _____.

8. The repetitive singing style in which a leader is imitated by a group of followers is called _____. In which musical cultures is this style common? _____

9. The structural procedure whereby a short pattern—melodic, rhythmic, or harmonic—is repeated is called _____.

10. The sections of a large-scale work are called _____.

11. Review the illustration on page 33 of the text that shows binary and ternary form in architecture. Describe other instances in which both forms, either natural or manufactured, are found in our lives. Remember that ternary is not just a three-part form but a symmetrical one, reflecting a departure or contrasting middle section followed by a return to the opening.

_____

_____

_____

_____

_____

Consider the melody of the traditional song *Yankee Doodle* ♪, then answer questions 12–17.

12. How many musical phrases are shown in this melody?

___ 1 ___ 2 ___ 3 ___ 4

13. Are they symmetrical (the same length musically)? _____

14. Does the second phrase (beginning in measure 5) provide:

___ repetition ___ contrast ___ variation

15. Consider the third phrase (in measure 9). Does it provide:

___ repetition ___ contrast ___ variation

16. Compare the melodic contour of measures 9 and 13. What technique is used here?

___ literal repetition ___ sequence

17. Is this tune best described as:

___ binary form ___ ternary form

5. *Review* Elements of Music: Tempo and Dynamics
Chap. 6 Chr/Sh/Std

Terms to Remember

tempo	tempo (continued)	dynamics
accelerando	*moderato*	*crescendo*
adagio	*molto*	*decrescendo*
allegro	*non troppo*	*diminuendo*
andante	*poco*	*forte*
a tempo	*presto*	*fortissimo*
grave	*ritardando*	*mezzo piano*
largo	*vivace*	*mezzo forte*
meno		*piano*
		pianissimo
		sforzando

Exercises

Complete the following questions.

1. The standard Italian term for a fast, cheerful tempo is _____.

2. The Italian modifier meaning "not too much" is _____.

3. What tempo is even faster than that of question 1?_____

4. A slow tempo at pace of walking is _____

5. The indication to become gradually slower is_____;

   to become gradually faster is _____.

6. A return to the original tempo would be indicated_____.

7. A tempo marking of *poco a poco adagio* means _____.

8. A tempo of *molto vivace* would be best translated as _____.

9. The dynamic marking for soft is_____ and for loud, _____.

10. Growing gradually louder would be indicated by _____;

    growing gradually softer is indicated by _____.

11. A sudden stress or accent might be called for by a _____.

True or False

_____ 12. Dynamics in music can affect our emotional reactions.

_____ 13. Nineteenth-century musical scores generally lack indications for
          dynamics or tempo.

_____ 14. A change in volume from **mp** to **f** would be indicated by a
     diminuendo.

_____ 15. The softest dynamic marking ever used is **pp**.

_____ 16. Tempo and dynamics contribute to the overall musical expression
     of a piece.

Consider the musical score below from Clara Schumann's Scherzo, Op. 10,
a solo piano work we will study later, and answer the following questions
about the tempo and dynamic markings in the music. You can listen to this
work on your CD set.

17. Which term indicates the tempo? _____ What does this

    term mean? _____

18. What is the first dynamic marking? _____ What does it mean?

    _____

19. Where does the dynamic (volume) level change? _____

    What does it change to? _____

20. What is the sign (>——) called? _____ What kind of

    change does it indicate? _____

21. At the end of the second line, the marking **sf** means _____,

    indicating the pianist should _____.

> ### 6. *Review* World Musical Instruments, Ensembles, and Their Context
> **Chaps.** 7–10 Chr/Sh/Std

Exercises

Match the following instruments with their category of sound production (use choices as many times as needed).

_____ 1. gourd rattle

_____ 2. Japanese koto

_____ 3. bagpipe

_____ 4. Indian sitar

_____ 5. African hand drum

_____ 6. gong

a. aerophone

b. chordophone

c. idiophone

d. membranophone

Complete the following questions.

7. In which instrument category do horns and flutes fall? _____

8. The instrument category that produces sound from the substance of the instrument as it is rubbed, struck, or shaken is _____.

9. _____ describes any instrument that is sounded from a tightly stretched skin that is struck, rubbed, or plucked.

10. _____ describes an instrument that produces sound from a vibrating string stretched between two points. It can be sounded by two means: _____ and _____.

11. Name two modern Western instruments of Middle Eastern origin:

a. _____ b. _____

True or False

_____ 12. The gong is widely used throughout Africa.

_____ 13. Members of the xylophone family are used in Southeast Asia and Africa.

_____ 14. Trumpets and horns were used in the ancient world.

_____ 15. The tom-tom is a type of gong of African origin.

_____ 16. Chamber groups combining strings and percussion are common in India.

_____ 17. The gamelan is a type of orchestra in Indonesia.

_____ 18. Gagaku is the name of an African drum.

_____ 19. Turkish Janissary bands made use of wind and percussion instruments.

_____ 20. All ensembles around the world make use of a conductor.

_____ 21. In some cultures, women's voices are preferred for certain styles of music.

_____ 22. A koto is a bowed string instrument from India.

_____ 23. The sitar is used in classical music from India.

_____ 24. Music serves different functions in different societies.

_____ 25. Musical genres, or categories of music, are the same in all societies.

_____ 26. Vocal timbre, or tone quality, varies from culture to culture, based on differing preferences.

_____ 27. In modern times, all music is notated, or written down.

_____ 28. Oral transmission involves performance without notation.

_____ 29. Classical (art) music is never influenced by traditional or popular music.

_____ 30. Crossover refers to a kind of music notation.

31. Locate a recording (in the library or on the Internet) of a Japanese koto or Indian sitar, listen to several selections, then describe the sound of the instrument below.
(Use the recording notes to help you answer the following questions.)

Recording title: _____

Instrument(s): _____

Description: _____

_____

_____

_____

Is this ___ traditional, ___ popular, or ___ classical music?

What function does this style play in its native society?

_____

_____

_____

7. *Review* Western Orchestral Instruments
Chap. 8 Chr/Sh/Std

Exercises

Identify each of the instruments pictured below in four ways: its name, chosen from column I; its instrument family, from column II; its means of sound production, from column III; and its world instrument category, from column IV.

I. INSTRUMENT
- a. bassoon
- b. clarinet
- c. double bass
- d. flute
- e. French horn
- f. oboe
- g. saxophone
- h. timpani
- i. trombone
- j. trumpet
- k. tuba
- l. violin

II. FAMILY
- m. brass
- n. percussion
- o. strings
- p. woodwinds

III. SOUND PRODUCTION
- q. blown double reed
- r. blown single reed
- s. bowed string
- t. struck with mallets
- u. air column divided across hole
- v. lips buzzing into mouthpiece

IV. CATEGORY
- w. aerophones
- x. chordophones
- y. idiophones
- z. membranophones

(Sample)

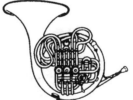

1. Instrument: _l_
   Family: _o_
   Production: _s_
   Category: _x_

2. Instrument: ___
   Family: ___
   Production: ___
   Category: ___

3. Instrument: ___
   Family: ___
   Production: ___
   Category: ___

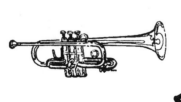

4. Instrument: ___
   Family: ___
   Production: ___
   Category: ___

5. Instrument: ___
   Family: ___
   Production: ___
   Category: ___

6. Instrument: ___
   Family: ___
   Production: ___
   Category: ___

7. Instrument: ___
   Family: ___
   Production: ___
   Category: ___

8. Instrument: ___
   Family: ___
   Production: ___
   Category: ___

9. Instrument: ___
   Family: ___
   Production: ___
   Category: ___

10. Instrument: ___
    Family: ___
    Production: ___
    Category: ___

11. Instrument: ___
    Family: ___
    Production: ___
    Category: ___

12. Instrument: ___
    Family: ___
    Production: ___
    Category: ___

13. Which instruments do you find are difficult to tell apart?

_____

14. Which do you find easy to distinguish?

_____

There are several pieces of music that feature the sounds of the instruments (in addition to Britten's *The Young Person's Guide to the Orchestra*, discussed in Chapter 9 and Listening Guide 1). One of these is Sergei Prokofiev's *Peter and the Wolf*. Locate a recording of this composition in the library.

15. Listen to this work, then describe the roles given to the instruments.

_____

_____

_____

_____

_____

8. *Review* Musical Instruments and Ensembles
Chaps. 7–9 Chr/Sh/Std

Terms to Remember

a cappella	jazz band	plucked
alto	madrigal choir	register
baritone	mezzo-soprano	soprano
bass	orchestra	string quartet
bowed	organ	synthesizer
chamber music	part songs	tenor
concert band	piano	timbre
conductor	piano quartet	unpitched
duration	pitch	volume
embouchure	pitched	woodwind quintet

Exercises

Complete the following questions.

1. The four qualities of any musical sound are _____,

   _____, _____, and _____.

2. The distinctive sound of each instrument is its _____.

3. List the three standard voice parts for women (highest to lowest).

   _____ _____ _____

4. List the three standard voice parts for men (highest to lowest).

   _____ _____ _____

5. The two categories of orchestral string instruments, grouped by the

   way they are played, are _____ and _____.

   Name an instrument for each: _____ and _____

6. The two categories of percussion instruments are _____ and

   _____. Examples: _____ and _____

7. The lips, lower facial muscles, and jaw are referred to as a wind player's

   _____.

8. _____ refers to music sung without instrumental

   accompaniment.

9. The _____ is an instrument that produces sound via a keyboard

   mechanism that causes hammers to strike the strings.

10. "The king of instruments" produces sound from air flowing through its many pipes. What is it? _____

11. Small ensembles with one musician per part play _____.

12. The standard ensemble consisting of 2 violins, 1 viola, and 1 cello is known as a(n) _____.

13. A chamber ensemble that includes flute, oboe, clarinet, French horn, and bassoon is known as a(n) _____.

14. Name a chamber ensemble of piano and strings: _____.

15. A large musical ensemble made up predominantly of winds and percussion is the _____.

16. An ensemble made up of sections of reed, brass, and rhythm instruments that plays popular music is the _____.

17. The person who beats time to help keep large ensembles together is known as a(n) _____.

Match the following string effects with their definitions.

____ 18. pizzicato   a. a rapid alternation from one tone to the one above it

____ 19. trill   b. muffling the sound by a small attachment on the bridge

____ 20. vibrato   c. plucking the string with the finger

____ 21. muting   d. playing two notes at one time

____ 22. staccato   e. a slide on the string while bowing

____ 23. double stopping   f. a short, detached style of playing

____ 24. glissando   g. throbbing effect produced by slightly wiggling the finger while bowing

25. Watch a conductor in action (in a live performance or on a video or TV broadcast). Describe the conductor's hand motions and other body language in relation to the performance.

_____

_____

_____

_____

_____

> ### 9. *Listen* Britten's *The Young Person's Guide to the Orchestra*
> **LG** 1 Chr/Sh/Std

Exercises

Locate the recording of *The Young Person's Guide to the Orchestra* on your Resource CD. Follow Listening Guide 1 while listening, then answer the questions below.

THEME

1. What was Britten's source for the theme (main melody) of this work?

   _____

2. What instruments are heard in the original version of the theme♪ (this work is on your Resource CD as well)?

   _____

3. Describe the character of the theme in your own words.

   _____

4. How does the composer firmly establish this melody for the listener?

   _____

5. Can you differentiate between the sounds of each instrument family?

   _____ Describe in your own words the timbre or distinctive sound of each family below.

   Woodwinds: _____

   Brass: _____

   Strings: _____

   Percussion: _____

VARIATIONS

After the statements of the theme (principal melody) by each instrument family, Britten begins a series of variations on the theme.

6. How would you define a variation of a given melody?

   _____

7. Can you recognize the theme throughout the variations? _____

8. Can you distinguish the solo instrument over those that are playing the accompaniment?_____

9. Which woodwind instruments do you find easy to identify?

_____

Which are difficult? _____

10. Which string instruments do you find easy to identify?

_____

Which are difficult?_____

11. Which brass instruments do you find easy to identify?

_____

Which are difficult?_____

12. Of the percussion instruments heard, which have a definite pitch?

_____

13. Which are unpitched? _____

FUGUE

Use the last section of the work as a final review of the instruments. Here each instrument is heard in a very quick statement of a new theme or melody.

14. Knowing the range an instrument plays in will help you distinguish it from another family member whose timbre is similar. Arrange the instruments of each family from highest to lowest, as they are heard in both the variations and the fugue. Assign number 1 to the highest family member, 2 to the next highest, and so on.

___ bassoon	___ viola	___ French horn
___ piccolo	___ cello	___ tuba
___ clarinet	___ violin	___ trumpet
___ flute	___ double bass	___ trombone

15. How does Britten use imitation in this section of the piece?

_____

16. Where is the climax of the work? _____

_____

---

10. *Review* Style and Function in Music
Chap. 10 Chr/Sh/Std

Exercises

Complete the following questions.

1. What does the term "genre" mean? _____

   Name a literary genre (ex.: short story). _____

   Name a musical genre. _____

2. What distinguishes sacred music from secular music:?

   _____

   _____

3. What determines the style of any work of art?

   _____

4. Specifically, what determines the style of a musical work?

   _____

   _____

   _____

5. What are some factors that may make certain styles of non-Western
   music sound different or unfamiliar to Westerners?

   _____

   _____

   _____

   _____

6. Style is also what makes popular music sound different from classical
   music. List some types (categories) of popular music that you think
   represent differing styles.

   _____

   _____

   _____

   _____

7. Does the development of music in various world cultures follow the style periods of Western music? _____

Explain your answer. _____

_____

_____

8. Place the following Western style periods in chronological order by numbering them from 1 (the earliest) to 6 (the latest) in the left column. Give the approximate dates of each era in the right column.

ERA	DATES
____Baroque	_____
____Middle Ages	_____
____Romantic	_____
____Twentieth century	_____
____Classical	_____
____Renaissance	_____

9. Do the dates of musical periods coincide precisely with the dates of literary/artistic style periods? _____ yes _____ no

10. Why or why not?

_____

_____

_____

_____

Answer the following questions about this musical composition title:
Ludwig van Beethoven, Piano Sonata in C minor, Op. 13 (*Pathétique*)

11. The name of the composer is _____.

12. Which word tells us the performing medium for the work? _____

13. What is the genre for the work? _____

14. In what key is the work? _____

15. What is the cataloging number for the work? _____

16. What is the descriptive title (or nickname) for the work?

_____

11. *Explore* The Roles of Music around the World
CP 2 Chr/Sh/Std

Exercises

Complete the following questions.

1. Name some activities that might be performed while singing work songs.

   _____

2. Describe the responsorial singing style of work songs.

   _____

   _____

3. From what type of work song did blues and spirituals develop?

   _____

   _____

4. Can you name a folk song that might have originally been a work song?

   _____

5. What are some common traits of lullabies around the world?

   _____

   _____

6. In which meter are Western lullabies most often set? _____

   Why? _____

7. Name a lullaby that you have heard. _____

8. How is music used in worship services and what is its function?

   _____

   _____

9. Give examples of instruments or ensembles used to accompany

   military troops. _____

   _____

   _____

10. What is the name of the bugle call used to wake up the troops?

    _____ Have you heard this bugle call? _____ If so,

    where?_____

Listening Assignment

Locate a recording of African-American traditional songs or spirituals in your college library. Which songs do you think were used as work songs? Describe one or more of the songs that you think may have been sung during the work day and suggest which activities these might have accompanied. What feelings or emotions are conveyed in these songs?

Or visit the Web site (www.wwnorton.com/enjoy), read the Cultural Perspective, then describe below the path you chose through the Web links.

_____

_____

_____

_____

_____

_____

_____

_____

_____

_____

_____

_____

_____

_____

_____

_____

_____

_____

_____

_____

_____

_____

_____

_____

_____

---

12. *Review* Music in the Middle Ages
Chaps. 11–13 Chr/Sh; 52–54 Std

Exercises

SACRED MUSIC

True or False

_____ 1. Medieval monasteries played a central role in the preservation of knowledge from earlier cultures.

_____ 2. The church was especially important in shaping secular music of early times.

_____ 3. Hildegard of Bingen was an abbess who wrote church music.

_____ 4. Much music is left to us today from Greek and Roman civilizations.

_____ 5. The early music of the Christian church was influenced by Hebrew music.

_____ 6. Early musical notation, called neumes, developed as a memory tool for singers who learned chants orally.

_____ 7. The chants of the church used only the major and minor scale patterns found in later music.

_____ 8. The Mass of the Roman Catholic Church is celebrated daily and includes a Proper, which is appropriate to that feast, and the Ordinary, which remains the same for all feast days.

_____ 9. The Notre Dame School is renowned for early polyphonic writing called organum.

_____ 10. Léonin and Pérotin are important composers from the St. Peter's School of organum in Rome.

_____ 11. The cloistered life in the Middle Ages was open only to men.

_____ 12. People who entered religious orders led a demanding lifestyle.

Complete the following sentences.

13. The _____ is the most solemn service of the Roman Catholic Church.

14. The _____ are a series of services celebrated in religious institutions at various hours of the day.

15. The body of music for the Roman Catholic Church in the Middle Ages is called _____.

16. Medieval scale patterns used in Western music are called _____.

17. Music performed with exchanges between a soloist and chorus is said to be _____.

Match the following groups of musicians with descriptions below.

_____ 18. trouvères   a. female poet-musicians from France

_____ 19. troubadours   b. poet-musicians of northern France

_____ 20. jongleurs   c. German singers of courtly love

_____ 21. trobairitz   d. poet-musicians of southern France

_____ 22. Minnesingers   e. wandering actor-singers

Multiple Choice

_____ 23. The art of the troubadours and trouvères included:
   a. laments and love songs.
   b. political and war songs.
   c. dance songs.
   d. all of the above.

_____ 24. Which was NOT an activity associated with secular music in medieval society?
   a. dancing and dinner entertainment
   b. devotional services
   c. jousts and tournaments
   d. military and civic events

_____ 25. Which factor did NOT contribute significantly to the rise in the status of women in the Middle Ages?
   a. the cults of Marian worship
   b. the age of chivalry
   c. the love songs of court minstrels
   d. the attitudes of feudal society

26. What were the principal values during the age of chivalry? Which of these are valid today?

_____

_____

_____

27. Cite a popular song of today that echoes the sentiments of unrequited love heard in medieval songs.

_____

_____

13. *Explore* Music of the Muses
CP 3 Chr/Sh; 10 Std

Exercises

Complete the following questions.

1. How old are the oldest musical instruments? _____

2. Where is the so-called cradle of civilization? _____
_____

3. What are some of the earliest instruments known from ancient
   civilizations? _____

4. What are some of the musical instruments referred to in the Bible?
_____

5. What is the derivation of the word "music"? _____

6. Who are the Muses? _____
_____

7. What was the attitude of the Greeks toward music? _____
_____
_____

8. Which famous Greek thinkers studied the effects of music? _____
_____

9. What are the four subjects of the quadrivium? _____
_____

10. How did the Romans use music in their theatrical presentations?
_____
_____
_____

11. What type of instrument (string, brass, woodwind, percussion) is each
    of the following?

    timbrel _____

    aulos _____

    lyre _____

Essay

Read several of the Biblical references mentioned in this Cultural Perspective, then comment below on how music pervaded the lives of the Jews, as documented in the Hebrew scriptures (Old Testament).

Or visit the Web site (www.wwnorton.com/enjoy), read the Cultural Perspective, then describe below the path you chose through the Web links.

_____

_____

_____

_____

_____

_____

_____

_____

_____

_____

_____

_____

_____

_____

_____

_____

_____

_____

_____

_____

_____

_____

_____

_____

_____

---

14. *Listen* Hildegard of Bingen and Chant
*Gregorian Chant: Kyrie (**LG** 2 Chr; 34 Std; *e***LG**)
Hildegard of Bingen: *Alleluia, O virga mediatrix* (**LG** 3 Chr; 2 Sh; 35 Std; *e***LG**)

Exercises

Describe the musical characteristics of Gregorian chant:

1. Texture: _____

2. Rhythm/meter: _____

3. Type of movement: _____

4. Range: _____

5. Scale pattern: _____

6. From which service in the liturgy is the Kyrie? _____

7. What are the notational symbols for chant called? _____

Match the text setting terms with their correct definitions.

_____ 8. syllabic   a. many notes per syllable

_____ 9. neumatic   b. one note per syllable

_____ 10. melismatic   c. syllabic style with short melismas of 5 to
                              6 notes

*Listen to the Gregorian chant Kyrie while following the Listening Guide, then answer questions 11–16.

11. The Kyrie is a part of the_____ (Ordinary or Proper) of the Mass.

12. The text of the Kyrie is based on a _____ prayer.

13. The Kyrie consists of _____ phrases sung _____ times each.

14. The Kyrie is sung in a _____ style, alternating
    between a _____ and a _____.

15. The melody is _____ (conjunct or disjunct) and wavelike
    with a _____ (small, medium, or large) range that grows
    _____ (wider or narrower) in the second and third sections.

16. The text setting (relationship of notes to words) alternates between
    _____ and _____.

Listen to Hildegard of Bingen's *Alleluia, O virga mediatrix* while following the Listening Guide, then answer questions 17–25.

17. For which liturgical occasion(s) was Hildegard's chant *Alleluia, O virga mediatrix* sung? _____

18. Who is praised in the text? _____

19. This chant is sung in alternation between a soloist and a chorus; this style is known as _____.

____ 20. Which term best describes the texture?
   a. monophonic
   b. polyphonic
   c. homophonic

____ 21. Which best describes the melodic movement of Hildegard's chant?
   a. completely conjunct
   b. mostly conjunct with a few leaps
   c. very disjunct

____ 22. Which best describes the text setting in *Alleluia, O virga mediatrix?*
   a. all syllabic
   b. mostly neumatic
   c. mostly melismatic

23. What musical characteristic(s) heard in this chant could be considered unique to the music of Hildegard?

   _____

   _____

   Cite an example in the chant where this characteristic is heard.

   _____

24. Cite a specific example of word painting in *Alleluia, O virga mediatrix.* What is the text (and translation) and how does Hildegard depict the word musically?

   _____

   _____

25. What unique qualities did Hildegard possess as an individual that allowed her to be famous in her own day?

   _____

   _____

   _____

   _____

---

15. *Listen* Organum and Motet

Notre Dame School Organum: *Gaude Maria virgo* (**LG** 4 Chr; 3 Sh; 36 Std; *e***LG**)
*Adam de la Halle: *Aucun se sont loé/A Dieu/Super te* (**LG** 5 Chr; 37 Std; *e***LG**)

Exercises

Listen to the Notre Dame School Organum *Gaude Maria virgo* while following the Listening Guide, then answer questions 1–12.

1. The earliest type of polyphony is called _____.

2. Polyphony brought about the use of _____, in which different voices sing together.

3. Composers of organum based their compositions on _____ _____.

4. Name two composers associated with the Notre Dame School.

   _____ and _____

   Where was this school of composition located? _____

   In which century(centuries) did it flourish? _____

5. Which composer is credited with writing the *Great Book of Organum*?

   _____

6. Which composer is sometimes credited with writing the organum *Gaude Maria virgo?*_____

7. The text of *Gaude Maria virgo* is in praise of _____ and would be sung for occasions celebrating _____.

8. The text setting alternates between _____ and _____, with _____ (how many?) voices singing rhythmically over a sustained bottom voice.

9. The bottom voice sings the _____ part in long notes.

10. The texture shifts from _____ at the beginning to _____.

11. The upper voices feature a repeated rhythmic pattern known as a _____.

    Describe the pattern you hear. _____

12. Can you hear the two moving upper parts? _____ How would you describe how they move? _____

    Can you hear the lowest voice ? _____ Is it easy or difficult to pick out? _____

*Listen to Adam de la Halle's *Aucun se sont loé/A Dieu/Super te* while following the Listening Guide, then answer questions 13–27.

True or False

_____ 13. The texture of this work is monophonic.

_____ 14. The genre of this work is a secular motet.

_____ 15. The upper voices sing the same text but in different languages.

_____ 16. The texts are based on French love poems.

_____ 17. The bottom voice is newly composed, with no pre-existent musical basis.

_____ 18. The tenor voice was often performed instrumentally.

_____ 19. This motet is in quadruple meter.

_____ 20. The tenor voice contains a repeated rhythmic pattern known as an ostinato.

_____ 21. The upper voices have simple rhythms that move as slowly as the tenor voice.

22. Describe briefly the origin of the motet. _____

    _____

    _____

23. What are the typical languages for motet texts? _____

24. Explain the term "polytextual" as it applies to the motet.

    _____

    _____

25. What is the subject of the top voice (triplum) text in this motet?

    _____

26. What is the subject of the middle voice (duplum) text?

    _____

27. What is the term for the bottom voice in a motet? _____

    What is the derivation of this word? _____

16. *Explore* Chant as Music for Worship
CP 4 Chr/Sh; 11 Std   𝑒

Exercises

Complete the following questions.

1. How would you define chant musically? _____

_____

2. How are the performances of the psalms similar in the early Judaic and
early Christian traditions? _____

_____

What is a cantor? _____

3. How are the sacred texts of the Koran presented in worship?

_____

4. How do the chants for private devotion and public performance differ
in Islamic worship? _____

_____

5. What is unusual about the vocal style of Tibetan chant?

_____

Which ensemble has popularized this style around the world?

_____ Which album by this group was recorded while on

a U.S. tour? _____

6. What is the acoustical meaning of the term "fundamental"?

_____

"Overtone"? _____

7. Describe the Afro-Cuban religion of Santeria.

_____

_____

How does the music for Santeria differ from chant?

_____

Listening Assignment

Find a recording of Jewish chant in your library (or ask your instructor for one from the Music Example Bank). Listen and compare its singing style and melodic characteristics with Gregorian chant (for example, Kyrie, on your recordings).

Or visit the Web site (www.wwnorton.com/enjoy), read the Cultural Perspective, then describe below the path you chose through the Web links.

_____

_____

_____

_____

_____

_____

_____

_____

_____

_____

_____

_____

_____

_____

_____

_____

_____

_____

_____

_____

_____

_____

_____

---

17. *Listen* Medieval Secular Music

Machaut: *Puis qu'en oubli* (**LG** 7 Chr; 4 Sh; 39 Std; *e***LG**)
*Moniot d'Arras: *Ce fut en mai* (**LG** 6 Chr; 38 Std; *e***LG**)
*Anonymous: *Royal estampie* No. 4 (**LG** 8 Chr; 40 Std; *e***LG**)

Exercises

Listen to the Machaut chanson *Puis qu'en oubli* while following the Listening Guide, then answer questions 1–14.

1. This work represents: ___ secular music ___ sacred music

2. The era it represents is: ___ Ars Antiqua ___ Ars Nova

3. The chanson's texture is: ___ monophonic ___ polyphonic

4. The chanson's structure is: ___ a fixed form ___freely composed

5. The chanson's text tells of: ___ unrequited love

___ praise of the Virgin Mary

6. The repeated text and music is called: ___ verse ___ refrain

7. In which form is this chanson? ___ ballade ___ rondeau

8. The setting is for: ___ 3 high voices ___ 3 low voices

9. How many different musical sections are heard? ___ 2 ___ 3

10. The meter of the chanson is: ___ duple ___ triple

11. The composer was: ___ a troubadour ___ a courtier and cleric

12. What accounts for the complexity you hear in this work?

_____

_____

13. What holds the work together structurally?_____

_____

_____

14. Describe the sentiment of courtly love expressed in the text.

_____

_____

_____

*Comparing two medieval secular works

      a. Moniot d'Arras: *Ce fut en mai*
      b. Anonymous: *Royal estampie* No. 4

Listen to the two works above, following the Listening Guides, then write the letter of the work(s) next to each characteristic that applies. More than one answer may be appropriate.

_____ 15. The form of the piece is a strophic chanson of five verses, each with an elaborate rhyme scheme.

_____ 16. Instrumental improvisation is central to the performance of this work.

_____ 17. This stately piece calls for elaborate body movements.

_____ 18. The work is a monophonic song that is often performed with improvised instrumental accompaniment.

_____ 19. The work can appropriately be performed with instruments of the loud or outdoor category.

_____ 20. The work is written by one of the last of the trouvères.

_____ 21. The work has a monophonic texture.

Early Instruments

_____ *22. Which group of instruments is featured in the *Royal estampie* No. 4?
      a. *bas* (soft)
      b. *haut* (loud)
      c. both *bas* and *haut*

_____ 23. The tabor is a:
      a. brass instrument.
      b. percussion instrument.
      c. woodwind instrument.

_____ 24. Instruments used for outdoor events were:
      a. *bas* (soft)
      b. *haut* (loud)
      c. *grand* (large)

  25. Which early instruments have modern counterparts? Which do not?

_____

_____

_____

_____

---

18. *Explore* Opening Doors to the East
CP 5 Chr/Sh; 12 Std

Exercises

Complete the following questions.

1. What was the purpose of the Crusades? _____

   _____

   In which centuries did they take place? _____

2. What modern geographical locale was the goal of the crusaders?

   _____

3. What military skills did Europeans learn from their enemies?

   _____

4. What types of knowledge were acquired from the Arab world?

   _____

   _____

5. Name three ways in which music was influenced by the Eastern world:

   a. _____

   b. _____

   c. _____

6. What Chinese ruler welcomed Marco Polo into his empire?

   _____ In which century?_____

7. What technical skills did Marco Polo and his explorers bring to western

   Europe from China? _____

   _____

8. What can we deduce from Polo's writings about the Tartars' use of

   music? _____

   _____

9. What religion was established in China during this era?

   _____

Essay

Discuss ways in which early historical encounters between Eastern and Western peoples contributed to the global awareness of today's society.

Or visit the Web site (www.wwnorton.com/enjoy), read the Cultural Perspective, then describe below the path you chose through the Web links.

19. *Review* The Renaissance Spirit
Chap. 14 Chr/Sh; 55 Std

Exercises

Check a or b

1. The Renaissance represents:
   ___ a. a sudden rebirth in learning and the arts
   ___ b. an increased awareness of the cultures of learned civilizations

2. The new era was characterized by:
   ___ a. an increased secular orientation
   ___ b. a complete religious orientation

3. The Renaissance was an age of:
   ___ a. scientific and intellectual inquiry
   ___ b. acceptance of faith and authority

4. This era found inspiration in:
   ___ a. the culture of the early Christian Church
   ___ b. the culture of ancient Greece and Rome

5. Check all those historical events that took place during the Renaissance.
   ___ a. the discovery of the New World
   ___ b. the invention of printing
   ___ c. the writing of the Magna Carta
   ___ d. the fall of the Roman Empire
   ___ e. the Protestant Reformation
   ___ f. the writing of the U.S. Constitution

6. Match the following well-known Renaissance personalities with their description.

   ____ Michelangelo   a. Italian scientist and astronomer

   ____ Machiavelli   b. Italian statesman

   ____ Galileo   c. Italian painter and sculptor

   ____ Martin Luther   d. English playwright

   ____ Shakespeare   e. German religious reformer

7. Name two great works of art created during the Renaissance.
   (Check text illustrations for examples.)

   ARTIST   WORK OF ART

   _____   _____

   _____   _____

8. The means by which musicians made their living in the Renaissance are similar to today's. For each of the following supporting institutions, list one specific use of music in the Renaissance and a parallel activity today.

	RENAISSANCE	MODERN-DAY
Church:	_____	_____
Civic:	_____	_____
Amateur music making:	_____	_____
Aristocratic courts:	_____	_____

9. What effect did the rise of a new middle class of merchants have on the commerce of music?

_____

_____

10. What roles did women play in music during the Renaissance era?

_____

_____

RENAISSANCE MUSICAL STYLE

True or False

_____ 11. The Renaissance saw the rise of solo instrumental music alongside the great vocal forms.

_____ 12. An *a cappella* performance of a vocal work might feature improvised instrumental accompaniment.

_____ 13. The predominant texture of Renaissance vocal music was imitative polyphony.

_____ 14. Expressive musical devices were frequently linked to the text in Renaissance music.

_____ 15. The use of a cantus firmus, or fixed melody, was abandoned in the Renaissance in favor of freer forms.

_____ 16. Renaissance music reflects a new taste for duple meter.

_____ 17. Renaissance music is characterized by the empty sonorities of open fourths and fifths.

---

20. *Explore* **When the Old World Meets the New World**
CP 6 Chr/Sh; 13 Std

Exercises

Complete the following questions.

1. During which historical era did Columbus explore the New World?

   _____

2. What musical characteristics did early explorers note about the singing

   of Native Americans? _____

   _____

3. What types of instruments did Europeans note were in use by

   Native Americans? _____

   _____

4. Name three functions that music played in Native American society.

   a. _____

   b. _____

   c. _____

5. Describe call-and-response singing. _____

   _____

   _____

6. What is a vocable?_____

7. Explain how music is preserved by oral tradition.

   _____

   _____

   _____

8. What music is preserved today through oral tradition?

   _____

   _____

Listening Assignment

Find an example of Native American ceremonial music (preferably an "authentic," or field, recording) in your college library (or ask your instructor for one from the Music Example Bank). Listen to it, and then describe the musical style in your own words. Consider vocal timbre, singing styles, melodic and rhythmic characteristics (range, shape, how it moves), and instruments used.

Or visit the Web site (www.wwnorton.com/enjoy), read the Cultural Perspective, and describe below the path you chose through the Web links.

_____

_____

_____

_____

_____

_____

_____

_____

_____

_____

_____

_____

_____

_____

_____

_____

_____

_____

_____

_____

_____

_____

21. *Review* Music in the Renaissance Era
Chaps. 15–16 Chr/Sh; 56–57 Std

Exercises

SACRED MUSIC

True or False

_____ 1. Which genre of music was generally NOT sung in the Roman Catholic Church?
   a. chansons
   b. motets
   c. Masses

_____ 2. Which of the following makes up the Ordinary of the Mass?
   a. Introit, Gradual, Communion, Ite missa est
   b. Kyrie, Gloria, Credo, Sanctus, Agnus Dei, Ite missa est
   c. Kyrie, Gloria, Collect, Epistle, Gradual, Canon

_____ 3. Which of the following movements of the Mass have three-part text and musical structures?
   a. Kyrie and Gloria
   b. Sanctus and Agnus Dei
   c. Kyrie and Agnus Dei

_____ 4. Which of the following characteristics is NOT typical of the Renaissance motet?
   a. multi-voiced, sometimes based on a chant
   b. Latin texts, often in praise of the Virgin Mary
   c. monophonic, and sung in the vernacular

_____ 5. Which of the following was NOT recommended by the Council of Trent?
   a. remove secularisms from church music
   b. use more instruments in church music
   c. make the words more understandable

_____ 6. The Catholic Church's reform movement toward piety was:
   a. the Reformation.
   b. the Counter-Reformation.
   c. the Ordinary.

True or False

_____ 7. Du Fay used cantus firmus technique in his Masses.

_____ 8. Josquin spent his entire productive career in northern Europe.

_____ 9. Palestrina's patrons included several popes.

_____ 10. Palestrina was a Burgundian composer.

_____ 11. Renaissance composers often set the Ordinary of the Mass polyphonically..

41

True or False

____ 12. The principal forms of Renaissance secular music were the chanson and the motet.

____ 13. Women were barred from secular music making in the Renaissance.

____ 14. The madrigal flourished principally in France.

____ 15. The English madrigal was generally more serious and complex than its Italian counterpart.

____ 16. The texts of the chanson and the madrigal dealt largely with love, both courtly and rustic, and were written in the vernacular (language of the people).

____ 17. Instrumental music making was a feature of home life.

____ 18. Instruments were used exclusively for the dance and never with voices in the Renaissance.

____ 19. Specific instruments were rarely called for in Renaissance music.

____ 20. Instruments were divided into loud and soft categories, their use based on the occasion.

____ 21. Monteverdi contributed significantly to the development of the Italian madrigal.

____ 22. Word painting is an expressive feature used in madrigals.

Match the dance types below with the correct description.

____ 23. pavane   a. an Italian jumping dance

____ 24. gagliard   b. a German dance in moderate duple meter

____ 25. allemande   c. a slow, stately processional dance

____ 26. saltarello   d. a quick French dance

27. What was the *Concerto delle donne?*

_____

28. What was new and remarkable about their singing style?

_____

_____

_____

---

22. *Listen* Renaissance Sacred Music

*Du Fay: *L'homme armé* Mass, Kyrie (**LG** 9 Chr; 41 Std; *e***LG**)
 Josquin: *Ave Maria . . . virgo serena* (**LG** 10 Chr; 5 Sh; 42 Std; *e***LG**)
 Palestrina: *Pope Marcellus* Mass, Gloria (**LG** 11 Chr; 6 Sh; 43 Std; *e***LG**)

Exercises

*Listen to the early-Renaissance Mass movement by Du Fay, then answer questions 1–9.

1. For how many voice parts is this Mass set? _____

2. The Kyrie is the first musical movement of the _____ of the Mass.

3. What is the cantus firmus (fixed song) on which this Mass is set?

   _____

   Can you hear the cantus firmus in the work? _____

4. What is the overall form of the movement? _____

5. How does the text contribute to shaping the form? _____

   _____

6. What is the predominant texture of the movement? _____

   _____

7. In which meter is this movement set? _____

8. Does the harmony sound hollow or full? _____

9. Why did the Catholic Church object to masses such as this one later in the sixteenth century?

   _____

   _____

Listen to the Josquin motet while following the Listening Guide, then answer questions 10–18.

10. For how many voices is this work set? _____

11. Whose virtues are praised in its text?_____

12. Describe the structure of the text. _____

   _____

13. In which language is the text written? _____

14. What textures does Josquin employ to set off the different sections of

   the text? _____

15. Is this work _____ based on a chant or _____ freely composed?

    Explain. _____

    _____

16. Does this recording use _____ male voices only or _____ mixed voices?

    What voices would have been used in the Renaissance? _____

17. Is this work performed _____ *a cappella* _____ with accompaniment?

18. Would you say that Josquin's first priority was the music or text in this

    work? _____ Explain your answer. _____

    _____

Listen to the Palestrina Mass movement while following the Listening Guide, then answer questions 19–29.

19. Is this movement part of the Mass? _____ Ordinary or _____ Proper?

20. For how many voice parts is the Mass written? _____

21. How does Palestrina create contrast in the voices and ranges heard?

    _____

    _____

22. Was this Mass originally sung by _____ male voices or _____ mixed voices?

    Explain. _____

    _____

23. Is this work performed _____ *a cappella* _____ with instruments?

24. Is its harmony best described as _____ consonant or _____ dissonant?

25. Is its texture more _____ homophonic or _____ polyphonic?

26. Is its meter _____ duple or _____ triple?

27. How does Palestrina make the text clear and audible? _____

    _____

28. What musical concerns of the Council of Trent did Palestrina try to

    meet in this work? _____

    _____

29. Comparing this work with the Josquin motet *Ave Maria . . . virgo serena,*

    which sounds more modern to you? _____

    Explain your answer. _____

    _____

> ### 23. *Listen* Sixteenth-Century Secular Music
> *Josquin: *Mille regretz* (**LG** 12 Chr; 44 Std; *e***LG**)
> *Susato: Pavane *Mille regretz* (**LG** 13 Chr; 45 Std; *e***LG**)
> *Monteverdi: *A un giro sol* (**LG** 14 Chr; 46 Std; *e***LG**)
> Farmer: *Fair Phyllis* (**LG** 15 Chr; 7 Sh; 47 Std; *e***LG**)

Exercises

*Listen to the Josquin chanson *Mille regretz* and the Susato dance based on it while following the Listening Guides, then answer questions 1–8 about these two secular works.

1. In which language is Josquin's *Mille regretz* set? _____

2. What is the subject of its text? _____

   _____

3. What makes this chanson sound sad and archaic? _____

   _____

4. Describe how the composer varies the texture in *Mille regretz*. _____

   _____

5. For how many voices is *Mille regretz* set? _____

6. What type of dance does Susato's *Mille regretz* represent? _____

   From which collection is it taken? _____

7. Which instruments are heard in this performance of the dance *Mille regretz*? _____

8. How does the texture differ in this instrumental dance from the vocal model? _____

THE MADRIGAL

*Listen to Monteverdi's madrigal *A un giro sol* while following the Listening Guide in the text, then answer questions 9–13.

9. In which country did the madrigal originate? _____

10. Cite a clear example of word painting in the Monteverdi madrigal.

    _____

    _____

    _____

11. How is dissonance used as an expressive device in this madrigal?

    _____

12. For how many voice parts is Monteverdi's *A un giro sol* written? _____

    Which parts (SATB)? _____

    What is the effect of this voicing? _____

    _____

13. Where does this work fall in the output of madrigals by Monteverdi?

    _____

Listen to Farmer's madrigal *Fair Phyllis* while following the Listening Guide in the text, then answer questions 14–19.

14. For how many voice parts is *Fair Phyllis* written? _____

    Which parts? _____

15. Cite an example of clear word painting in *Fair Phyllis*?

    _____

    _____

16. Describe why this madrigal might be considered rustic or pastoral.

    _____

    _____

17. Listen for the brief change to triple meter in *Fair Phyllis*. What is its

    musical effect? _____

18. How did the English madrigal differ from the Italian madrigal?

    _____

    _____

    _____

19. Consider a contemporary love song (a ballad, a Broadway musical selection, or a rock song). Describe below how the musical style supports the text. Are there examples of word painting in the modern piece?

    Selection: _____

    Description: _____

    _____

    _____

    _____

    _____

24. *Review* Transition to the Baroque
Trans. I Chr/Sh; II Std

Exercises

Fill in the answers below.

1. Giovanni Gabrieli was active as a composer at St. Mark's in (city)

   _____.

2. One important characteristic of music at St. Mark's was the use of two

   or three choirs, called _____ singing.

3. The use of these choirs in alternation and then together is a singing

   style known as _____.

4. This style marked a change from the predominantly polyphonic texture

   of the Renaissance to a more _____ texture, in which

   the words could better be understood.

For each of the traits listed below, indicate with the appropriate letter the
style to which it relates.

      a. Renaissance style
      b. Baroque style

_____ 5. precise instruments specified

_____ 6. modal harmony predominant

_____ 7. *a cappella* vocal performance

_____ 8. solo singing (monody) prevalent

_____ 9. use of cantus firmus structures

_____ 10. rise of opera and cantata

_____ 11. chanson and madrigal as major secular forms

_____ 12. establishment of major/minor tonality

_____ 13. rise of public theaters

_____ 14. sonata and concerto as important instrumental forms

_____ 15. dance music derived from vocal works

*Listen to Gabrieli's motet *O quam suavis* (**LG** 16 Chr; 48 Std; *e***LG**) while following the Listening Guide, then answer questions 16–21.

16. What innovations in instrumental music are credited to Giovanni Gabrieli?

_____

_____

_____

17. How does Gabrieli achieve dynamic contrasts in the motet *O quam suavis?*

_____

_____

_____

18. What musical forces (voices and instruments) were used to perform *O quam suavis?*

_____

_____

19. Is the text clearly heard in this work? _____

    Explain your answer. _____

20. Do you hear the shifts from duple to triple meter? _____

    What musical effect do they have? _____

_____

_____

21. What is the text of *O quam suavis* about? _____

_____

_____

    On which religious occasion was it sung? _____

_____

25. *Review* The Organization of Musical Sounds
Chaps. 17–18 Chr/Sh; 37–38 Std

Terms to Remember

key	octave
scale	half step/whole step
chromatic	transposition
diatonic	modulation
major	chords, active and rest
minor	triad
heptatonic	tonic
pentatonic	dominant
tritonic	subdominant
mode	microtone
tonality	raga

Exercises

Complete the following questions.

1. The division of the _____ is variable in musics around the world.

   In Western music, it is divided into _____ equal half steps.

2. How many half steps make up a whole step? _____

3. The distance between C and D is a(n) _____.

4. How many half steps make up the chromatic scale? _____

5. _____ refers to the principle of organization whereby we hear a piece of music in relation to a central tone.

6. The symbol to raise a pitch a half step is a _____ (shown as ____).

7. On the chart below, mark on top the intervals (W for whole step and H for half step) for a major scale, and on the bottom those for a minor scale.

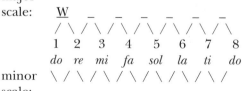

```
major
scale:   W   _   _   _   _   _   _   _
        / \ / \ / \ / \ / \ / \ / \
         1   2   3   4   5   6   7   8
        do  re  mi  fa  sol la  ti  do
minor   \ / \ / \ / \ / \ / \ / \ /
scale:
```

8. _____ refers to music built on the seven tones of a major or minor scale. It is best associated with music of the _____ era.

9. _____ refers to music built on all the half steps in the octave. It can best be associated with music of the _____ era.

10. _____ refers to a three-note scale, commonly used in certain musics of _____ (continent).

11. A five-note scale is referred to as _____ and is commonly heard in musics of _____ (cultures).

12. What is a microtone? _____

_____

13. How do Western listeners typically react to microtones?

_____

14. How is a raga different from a scale? _____

_____

Where are ragas used? _____

15. A three-note chord built on alternate scale tones is called a(n) _____. When built on the first scale tone, it is called a(n) _____ chord; when built on the fourth scale tone, it is called a _____ chord; and when built on the fifth scale tone, it is called a(n) _____ chord.

16. The shifting of all the tones of a melody by a uniform distance is called _____.

17. _____ refers to the passing from one key center to another within a composition.

18. Define active and rest chords and describe how they function.

_____

_____

_____

_____

---

26. *Review* The Baroque and the Arts
Chaps. 19–20 Chr/Sh; 58–59 Std

Exercises

Briefly characterize each of the following in the Baroque.

1. State of science: _____

_____

 Name a scientist from this era. _____

2. Focus of political power: _____

_____

 Name a head of state from this era. _____

3. Religious environment: _____

_____

 What regions of Europe were Protestant? _____

_____

4. Style of painting: _____

_____

 Name an artist from this era. _____

Multiple Choice

_____ 5. The origin of the term "Baroque" is probably:
  a. German, referring to something broken.
  b. Portuguese, referring to an irregularly shaped pearl.
  c. French, referring to a barge-type boat.

_____ 6. The university-based music ensemble that arose in the Baroque era is the:
  a. concert band.
  b. collegium musicum.
  c. madrigal choir.

Complete the following.

7. Opera had its origins in the experiments of a group known as the

_____.

8. The new style of music, or *le nuove musiche*, which features solo singing

with instrumental accompaniment, is called _____.

9. The new accompaniment style was performed on a group of
_____ instruments whose players read from a
shorthand notation known as _____.

10. The belief that words and music were closely linked is reflected in the
_____.

11. The rise in opera was responsible for the popularity of the voice of the
_____, a male singer whose high register was preserved
through an operation at an early age.

12. The tuning system developed during the Baroque that increased the
range of harmonic possibilities was
_____.

13. Name several musical devices used for emotional expression in Baroque
music. _____

14. What was the importance of the establishment of major/minor tonality
in the Baroque? _____
_____
_____

15. What role did improvisation play in Baroque music? Who was expected
to improvise? _____
_____
_____

16. What circumstances brought about an increased virtuosity in music?
_____
_____
_____

---

27. *Explore* Music and the Religious Spirit in the New World
CP 7 Chr/Sh; 14 Std

Exercises

Complete the following questions.

1. In the seventeenth century, what religion was predominant along the
   eastern seaboard of the United States? _____
   In northeastern Canada? _____ In Mexico? _____

2. What was the first book printed in the American colonies?

   _____

3. Describe the singing style known as "lining out."

   _____

   _____

4. When several embellished versions of the same melody occur
   simultaneously, we call this texture _____.

5. Name an important eighteenth-century American music teacher and
   composer. _____

6. What is a fuging tune? _____

   _____

7. What types of devotional music were sung in the nineteenth century?

   _____

   _____

   Was this music of African Americans, whites, or both?

   _____

8. Describe gospel music. _____

   _____

   _____

9. What is contemporary Christian music? _____

   _____

Listening Assignment

Find a recording of twentieth-century devotional music (spiritual, gospel, or contemporary Christian or Jewish music) in your college library (or ask your instructor for one from the Music Example Bank). Listen to a selection and describe its musical style (melody, rhythm, harmony, texture, form, tempo) and how it delivers its religious message.

Or visit the Web site (www.wwnorton.com/enjoy), read the Cultural Perspective, and describe below the path you chose through the Web links.

_____

_____

_____

_____

_____

_____

_____

_____

_____

_____

_____

_____

_____

_____

_____

_____

_____

_____

_____

_____

_____

_____

_____

_____

_____

_____

_____

_____

---

28. *Review* Baroque Vocal Forms
Chaps. 21–24 Chr/Sh; 60–63 Std

Exercises

Fill in the answers below.

1. The text of an opera is called the _____ and is written

   by a(n) _____.

2. Operas frequently open with an instrumental introduction called a(n)

   _____.

3. Opera soloists are generally featured in two types of works: a lyrical song

   that allows for emotional expression, called a(n) _____,

   and a disjunct song whose rhythm is fitted to the inflection of the text,

   called a(n) _____.

4. The term "secco" means _____, while the term

   "accompagnato" means _____. Both refer to

   types of _____.

5. An operatic song in the form **ABA**, which allows for the soloist to

   embellish the last section, is called a(n) _____.

6. The most important early Italian composer of operas was

   _____. His first opera was

   _____.

7. The Italian _____ was a vocal genre for solo singers and

   instrumental accompaniment, set to lyric, dramatic, or narrative poetry.

8. The master of the Baroque oratorio in England was _____.

   His most famous oratorio is _____.

True or False

_____ 9. Tragédie lyrique was a French opera style associated with Lully.

_____ 10. An oratorio is a secular stage work, with sets, costumes, and
        dramatic action.

_____ 11. The earliest opera plots were drawn from mythology.

_____ 12. The cantata is a multi-movement work that features solo vocalists,
        chorus, and orchestra.

____ 13. The cantata was central to the service of the Roman Catholic Church.

____ 14. The masque was a forerunner of the cantata in England.

____ 15. Many of Bach's cantatas are based on Protestant chorale or hymn tunes.

____ 16. The oratorio features arias, recitatives, and choruses among its sections.

____ 17. Cantatas may be based on either secular or sacred subjects.

____ 18. Opera seria was Italian comic opera.

____ 19. Women were not allowed to sing in opera productions.

____ 20. Barbara Strozzi was a renowned early Baroque composer and singer.

21. What differentiates an opera from an oratorio?

_____

_____

_____

_____

_____

22. What differentiates a cantata from an oratorio?

_____

_____

_____

_____

_____

29. *Listen* Baroque Opera and the Italian Cantata

*Monteverdi: *The Coronation of Poppea*, excerpt (**LG** 17 Chr; 49 Std; *e*LG)
  Purcell: *Dido and Aeneas*, Dido's Lament (**LG** 18 Chr; 8 Sh; 50 Std; *e*LG)
  Strozzi: *Begli occhi* (**LG** 19 Chr; 9 Sh; 51 Std; *e*LG)

Exercises

*Listen to the Monteverdi opera excerpt while following the Listening Guide, then answer questions 1–11.

1. What is the basis for the libretto of *The Coronation of Poppea?*

_____

2. How does the composer portray real human emotions through music?

_____

_____

3. Describe the singing style of the chorus during the coronation.

_____

_____

4. What instruments are heard in the sinfonia? _____

_____

5. What is the form of the final aria (duet)? _____

6. What is its structural basis? _____

   Can you hear this throughout? _____

7. What is the "affection" delivered by this aria? _____

8. How does the composer use dissonance for expression?

_____

9. From which period of Monteverdi's life does this opera originate?

_____

10. What was Monteverdi's first opera? _____

11. What was the basis for its plot? _____

Listen to the final scene from the Purcell opera *Dido and Aeneas* while following the Listening Guide, then answer questions 12–19.

12. Where was Purcell teaching when he wrote *Dido and Aeneas?*

_____

57

13. What is the basis of the libretto for *Dido and Aeneas?* _____

_____

14. Describe the style of the recitative "Thy hand, Belinda."

_____

_____

15. What is the structural basis for Dido's aria? _____

_____

Can you hear this throughout? _____

16. How does Purcell use chromaticism as an expressive device?

_____

17. The aria is in two main sections (binary). What is the text where the
second section begins? _____

18. Where does the aria reach a melodic and emotional climax?

_____

19. Could this love story (or that of Monteverdi's *The Coronation of Poppea*) be
updated to a modern-day movie or soap opera? Support your answer.

_____

_____

Listen to the Strozzi cantata *Begli occhi* while following the Listening Guide;
then answer questions 20–25.

20. What are the performing forces for Strozzi's cantata *Begli occhi?*

_____

21. How would you characterize the tempo and rhythmic movement in
Begli occhi? _____

22. What is the subject of the poem *Begli occhi?* _____

_____

23. What specific musical techniques does Strozzi employ to depict the
cantata text? _____

_____

24. Describe the role Barbara Strozzi played in the intellectual academies
of Venice. _____

_____

25. In which musical genres did she compose? _____

---

30. *Listen* **Bach and the Lutheran Cantata**

Bach: Cantata No. 80, *A Mighty Fortress Is Our God*, excerpts (**LG** 20 Chr; 10 Sh; 52 Std; *e***LG**)

Exercises

Listen to the Bach cantata excerpts while following the Listening Guide, read about it, then answer questions 1–13.

1. What is a chorale tune? _____

2. In a multi-voiced setting, in which voice is the chorale tune generally heard? _____

3. Who wrote the chorale text *Ein feste Burg ist unser Gott?*

   _____

4. How many movements do Bach's cantatas usually have? _____

5. How many movements does Cantata No. 80 have? _____

6. In how many movements does Bach use the chorale tune? _____

   Which movements? _____

7. What is the structure of the first movement of this cantata?

   _____

   Can you easily hear the chorale tune in this setting? _____

*8. What is the structure of the second movement, and where is the chorale tune heard? _____

   _____

*9. What is the "affection" or emotion communicated by this movement (consider its text as well as music)? _____

*10. Compare the use of the chorale in the first and fifth movements. In which is it most prominently heard? _____

   _____

   _____

11. How do the trumpets and timpani contribute to the work? When were these parts added? _____

   _____

   _____

59

12. What is the primary texture heard in the last (eighth) movement?

_____

13. In which voice part is the chorale tune heard in the last movement?

_____ Can you hear it clearly? _____

14. What was the religious occasion for this cantata?

_____

15. Were you familiar with the chorale tune *A Mighty Fortress Is Our God*

before you heard this work? _____

If yes, where did you learn it? _____

ABOUT THE COMPOSER

16. What were Bach's three important positions, and what kind of music did he write in each?

1st period: _____

_____

2nd period: _____

_____

3rd period: _____

_____

17. What is his most important collection of keyboard works?

_____

18. In which sacred genres did Bach compose? _____

_____

19. In which instrumental genres did he compose? _____

_____

20. What accounts, in your opinion, for Bach's continued popularity today?

_____

_____

_____

---

31. *Listen* Handel and the Oratorio
Handel: *Messiah,* excerpts (**LG** 21 Chr; 11 Sh; 53 Std; *e***LG**)

Exercises

Listen to the selections from *Messiah* while following the Listening Guide, then answer questions 1–10.

1. In which city was *Messiah* premiered? _____

2. What is the source of its text? _____

3. What are the subjects of the three principal sections of the oratorio?

   Part I: _____

   Part II: _____

   Part III: _____

4. What performing forces are required to perform *Messiah?*

   Instrumental: _____

   Vocal: _____

5. The first movement of *Messiah* is an orchestral introduction known as

   a(n) _____.

   What is its structure? _____

   _____

*6. Describe the difference heard in the two recitative styles of No. 14 from

   Messiah. _____

   _____

   _____

7. What is the structure of a da capo aria?_____

   Describe how the aria "Rejoice greatly" fits this structure.

   _____

   _____

   _____

61

8. Describe how Handel changes the texture throughout the *Hallelujah Chorus* as a means of contrast.

_____

_____

_____

9. Can you cite several examples of word or text painting in this oratorio (any movement)? _____

_____

_____

10. What do you think accounts for the continued popularity of this oratorio?

_____

_____

_____

_____

ABOUT THE COMPOSER

11. Where was Handel born? _____

12. What styles of opera did he write? _____

13. Where did he spend most of his career?_____

14. What London musical event changed the public's taste in opera?

_____

15. How did Handel respond to this change in taste?

_____

16. Name several biblical stories on which Handel based oratorios.

_____

17. What ailment did Handel and Bach both suffer late in life?

_____

32. *Review* Baroque Instrumental Forms
Chaps. 25–26 Chr/Sh; 64–65 Std

Exercises

Match the correct definitions with the following instrumental forms.

_____ 1. solo concerto

_____ 2. concerto grosso

_____ 3. fugue

_____ 4. prelude

_____ 5. suite

_____ 6. trio sonata

_____ 7. chorale prelude

_____ 8. passacaglia

_____ 9. French overture

_____ 10. Italian overture

a. a form based on a repeated bass line melody, or a ground bass

b. an organ work in which a traditional chorale tune is embellished

c. a short, continuous piece that often serves to introduce another movement

d. an orchestral introduction, in two repeated sections: slow and fast

e. a multi-movement form based on the opposition of one player against a larger group

f. a form based on the opposition of a small and large group

g. a series of dance movements, usually in the same key

h. a multi-movement work for two violins or other melody instruments and basso continuo

i. an orchestral introduction, in three sections: fast–slow–fast

j. a highly structured contrapuntal form, based on a single theme or subject

True or False

_____ 11. Vivaldi's *The Four Seasons* comprises four concertos, each based on a poem describing a season of the year.

_____ 12. Vivaldi is known principally for his vocal music.

_____ 13. The Baroque concerto is most often based on an orchestral refrain, or ritornello procedure.

_____ 14. The standard Baroque concerto has three movements.

_____ 15. A church sonata (*sonata da chiesa*) is a dance suite for full orchestra.

_____ 16. A suite is made up of dance movements, many of which are in binary form.

_____ 17. The piano was the most popular Baroque keyboard instrument.

_____ 18. The Italian composer Arcangelo Corelli established the trio sonata structure.

Multiple Choice

_____ 19. Which is NOT a standard dance in the Baroque suite?
  a. gigue
  b. minuet
  c. allemande

_____ 20. Binary form is best outlined as:
  a. **AB**.
  b. **ABA**.
  c. **ABC**.

_____ 21. The main theme of a fugue is known as the:
  a. episode.
  b. subject.
  c. fugato.

_____ 22. A passage in a fugal style within a nonfugal piece is called:
  a. stretto.
  b. dominant.
  c. fugato.

_____ 23. The answer in a fugue is:
  a. the main theme imitated at another pitch level.
  b. the opening section.
  c. overlapping entries of the main theme.

_____ 24. A section of a fugue in which the main theme is NOT heard is called a(n):
  a. exposition.
  b. episode.
  c. recapitulation.

_____ 24. Which texture best defines a fugue?
  a. homophonic
  b. heterophonic
  c. polyphonic

_____ 25. The word "fugue" is from the Latin word for:
  a. flight.
  b. fight.
  c. fidget.

_____ 26. Which is NOT an important Baroque composer of instrumental music?
  a. Georg Philipp Telemann
  b. Antonio Vivaldi
  c. Claudio Monteverdi

---

33. *Listen* The Baroque Sonata and Concerto
*Corelli: Trio Sonata, Op. 3, no. 2, Third and Fourth Movements (**LG** 22 Chr; 54 Std; *e***LG**)

Vivaldi: *Spring,* from *The Four Seasons* (**LG** 23 Chr; 12 Sh; 55 Std; *e***LG**)

*Bach: *Brandenburg Concerto* No. 2 in F major, First and Second Movements (**LG** 24 Chr; 56 Std; *e***LG**)

Exercises

*Listen to the Corelli Trio Sonata while following the Listening Guide, then answer questions 1–5.

1. The favored trio sonata combination in the Baroque was _____ and continuo.

2. How many movements does Corelli's Trio Sonata, Op. 3, no. 2, have? ____

3. What is the tempo scheme of the movements? _____

4. What dance type does the third movement resemble? _____

   Describe its musical character. _____

   _____

5. What dance type does the fourth movement resemble? _____

   Describe its musical character. _____

   _____

Listen to the concerto *Spring* (*La Primavera*) by Vivaldi while following the Listening Guide, then answer questions 6–15.

6. What are the two main types of concerto in the Baroque? _____

   _____

7. Which type is Vivaldi's *Spring?* _____

8. What is the order of movements (by tempo) in this concerto?

   _____

9. What extramusical material determines the form of the work?

   _____

10. What is a ritornello? _____

   _____

11. How many ritornellos are heard in the first movement? _____

12. How many solo episodes are heard? _____

65

13. Do you think Vivaldi was successful in portraying images of springtime? _____ Explain your answer. _____

_____

14. What elements makes this concerto virtuosic? _____

_____

15. Who were the performers that Vivaldi taught and for whom he wrote much of his instrumental music? _____

_____

*Listen to the first and second movements of Bach's *Brandenburg Concerto No. 2* while following the Listening Guide, then answer questions 16–26.

16. What type of concerto is this? _____

17. What is the concerto's overall structure? _____

_____

18. What is the full orchestra called? _____

19. What is the solo group called? _____

20. What instruments make up the solo group in this work?

_____

21. What gives the first movement its forward-moving energy?

_____

_____

22. How many ritornellos are heard in this movement? _____
    How do they unify the work? _____

_____

23. How does Bach provide contrast in this work? _____

_____

_____

24. Which solo instrument is omitted in the second movement? _____

25. How does the composer make this movement sound emotional?

_____

26. What is the history of the *Brandenburg Concertos*?

_____

_____

_____

---

34. *Listen* The Baroque Suite

Handel: *Water Music,* Suite in D major, *Allegro and *Alla hornpipe* (**LG** 25 Chr; 13 Sh; 57 Std; *e***LG**)

Exercises

Fill in the answers below.

1. The Baroque suite comprised a number of dances in the same key. List the four standard ones below, with country of origin and musical character.

   Dance _____ Country _____

   Character _____

   Dance _____ Country _____

   Character _____

   Dance _____ Country _____

   Character _____

   Dance _____ Country _____

   Character _____

2. List some dances that are frequently added to a suite?

   _____

3. Which Baroque composer wrote the suite entitled *Tafelmusik?*

   _____ What does this title mean? _____

   _____

Listen to the *Allegro and *Alla hornpipe* from Handel's *Water Music* while following the Listening Guide, then answer questions 4–15.

   *4. What is the form of the Allegro from the D-major suite in *Water Music?*

   _____

   *5. What instruments are featured in the fanfare opening?

   _____

   6. Where was the *Water Music* suite first performed?

   _____

   7. What instruments were lacking in this performance?

   _____

67

8. What is another well-known orchestral suite by Handel?

   _____

9. What is the meter of the *Alla hornpipe?* _____

10. What instruments are first heard in the dance? _____

11. What other instruments are featured during the movement?

    _____

12. What is the form of the hornpipe? _____

13. In the **B** Section, the harmony shifts from D major to B minor. Can you hear the difference? _____

14. What instruments are heard in the **B** Section? _____

    _____

15. Describe the timbre of some of the Baroque period instruments in this recording, noting how they differ from their modern counterparts.

    _____

    _____

    _____

    _____

    _____

    _____

---

35. *Listen* Baroque Keyboard Music
*Bach: Chorale Prelude, *A Mighty Fortress Is Our God* (**LG** 26 Chr; 58 Std; *e***LG**)
Bach: Prelude and Fugue in C minor, from *The Well-Tempered Clavier*, Book 1
(**LG** 27 Chr; 14 Sh; 59 Std; *e***LG**)

Exercises

*Listen to the Bach organ chorale prelude while following the Listening Guide, then answer questions 1–5.

1. What is the origin of the tune on which Bach based this work?

_____

Is it easily recognizable throughout? _____

2. What musical techniques does Bach use to manipulate the tune?

_____

3. How does an organ differ from a piano? _____

_____

4. How does the organ achieve different timbres, or colors?

_____

5. What role does the chorale prelude play in the Lutheran service?

_____

Listen to the Bach Prelude and Fugue in C minor while following the
Listening Guide, then answer questions 6–22.

6. Bach's collection *The Well-Tempered Clavier* includes _____ books of

keyboard works written for _____. Each book has

_____ preludes and fugues, each in a different major or minor key.

Thus there are a total of _____ preludes and fugues in the collection.

7. What is the main theme of the fugue called? _____

8. What is the first section of the fugue called, in which each voice is

heard with the theme? _____

9. What is an episode? _____

_____

How many are there in this fugue?_____

Match the following musical characteristics in *The Well-Tempered Clavier* with either

      a. the prelude or
      b. the fugue

____ 10. melodically oriented, with a theme that is heard repeatedly

____ 11. harmonically oriented, with chords establishing the motion

____ 12. a free, improvisational style

____ 13. a strict rhythmic pulse throughout

____ 14. form based on imitation

____ 15. linear movement with different "voices"

____ 16. a "perpetual motion" rhythmic drive

____ 17. largely homophonic texture

____ 18. largely polyphonic texture

19. Can you follow the form of the fugue from the line graph in the Listening Guide? _____

20. What is highly structured about a fugue? _____

_____

_____

21. What are some of the contrasts between the style of this C-minor prelude and the fugue that is paired with it?

_____

_____

_____

_____

22. Name three important Baroque keyboard instruments.

_____

36. *Review* From Baroque to Classical
Trans. II Chr/Sh; III Std

Exercises

Complete the following questions.

1. What does the word "Rococo" mean? _____

2. What are the major characteristics of Rococo art? _____

_____

Name a well-known painter of the era. _____

3. Name two French composers that represent this style.

_____

4. What traits were composers breaking away from in the Rococo?

_____

_____

5. What were the goals of the new "sensitive" style?

_____

6. What major instrumental genres were developed during this era?

_____

7. What was important about the premiere of *The Beggar's Opera?*

_____

_____

8. What brought on the "War of the Buffoons"?

_____

_____

9. What changes did Gluck wish to bring about in opera seria?

_____

_____

10. What type of subjects did Gluck explore in his operas?

_____

For each of the traits listed below, indicate with the appropriate letter the style to which it best relates.

        a. Baroque style
        b. Classical style

____ 11. polyphonic textures

____ 12. single "affection" for each work or movement

____ 13. symmetrical and balanced phrases

____ 14. forte/piano contrasts and echo effects

____ 15. improvisation limited to cadenzas

____ 16. symphony and string quartet prevalent

____ 17. organ and harpsichord as solo instruments

____ 18. use of chromatic harmony for expression

____ 19. piano as favored solo instrument

____ 20. use of clarinet in orchestra

____ 21. use of crescendos and decrescendos

22. Name the major composers of the Baroque era.

_____

Which of these did you know of prior to this course?

_____

23. Name the major composers of the Classical era.

_____

Which of these did you know of prior to this course?

_____

37. *Review* Focus on Form
Chaps. 27–28 Chr/Sh; 39–40 Std

Exercises

Fill in the answers below.

1. The smallest unit of a melody is called a(n) _____.

2. The principal melody in a composition is called a _____.

3. The manipulation and expansion of this melody is known as

_____.

4. Name several techniques through which musical material is developed.

_____

Multiple Choice

____ 5. How many movements are typically found in the multimovement
cycle?
a. one   c. four
b. two   d. six

____ 6. Which of the following genres is often in a multimovement cycle
form?
a. string quartet   c. sonata
b. symphony   d. all of the above

____ 7. Which of the following is the standard form for the first movement
in a multimovement cycle?
a. theme and variations form   c. minuet and trio form
b. sonata-allegro form   d. binary (**AB**) form

____ 8. Which are the three main sections of this first-movement form?
a. exposition–development–coda
b. exposition–development–recapitulation
c. minuet–trio–minuet
d. theme–variation 1–variation 2

____ 9. The section of a form that serves as a transition, often to another
key center, is known as a:
a. codetta.   c. bridge.
b. theme group.   d. development.

____ 10. The final section of a movement that rounds off the piece,
re-establishing the tonic key, is called the:
a. bridge.   c. introduction.
b. development.   d. coda.

____ 11. What is the standard tempo scheme of a multimovement cycle?
   a. fast–moderate–slow–fast   c. fast–slow–moderate–fast
   b. slow–fast–moderate–fast   d. fast–slow–fast–slow

12. Describe how the two principal themes of a sonata-allegro form differ from each other.

Theme (or theme group) 1   Theme (or theme group) 2

_____

_____

13. How does the final section or restatement of the above themes differ from what is heard in the exposition?

_____

_____

14. What is the purpose of the development section?

_____

_____

15. What elements can be varied in a theme and variations form?

_____

_____

True or False

____ 16. Minuet and trio form is most often found as the fourth movement of a sonata cycle.

____ 17. The minuet and trio form grew out of earlier dance forms.

____ 18. A minuet and trio is generally in duple meter.

____ 19. One type of rondo form can be outlined as **ABACABA**.

____ 20. A rondo features one main idea that keeps coming back throughout the work.

____ 21. A coda provides an introduction to a movement.

____ 22. Rounded binary form brings back the first theme at the close of the second section.

____ 23. Form is an important element in absolute music.

38. *Review* The Classical Spirit
Chaps. 29–30 Chr/Sh; 41–42 Std

Exercises

Fill in the answers below.

1. List general attributes of the Classical style that parallel those listed for the Romantic.

Classical   Romantic

a. _____   a. longing for strangeness,
   _____   ecstasy, and wonder

b. _____   b. intense subjectivity

c. _____   c. symbolized by Dionysus, God
   _____   of passion and intoxication

d. _____   d. uninhibited emotional
                                       expression

Choose the best answer for each.

_____ 2. Which historical event took place first?
   a. French Revolution
   b. American Revolution

_____ 3. Which culture was idealized in the eighteenth century?
   a. the medieval world
   b. the world of ancient Greece and Rome

_____ 4. Which eighteenth-century movement helped shape the modern world?
   a. the Protestant Reformation
   b. the Industrial Revolution

Match the following Classical-era figures with the correct description.

_____ 5. Friedrich von Schiller   a. French revolutionary painter

_____ 6. Thomas Jefferson   b. enlightened czarina of Russia

_____ 7. Jacques Louis David   c. principal author of the Declaration
                                        of Independence

_____ 8. Catherine the Great   d. English experimenter who invented
                                        the cotton gin

_____ 9. Eli Whitney   e. German early Romantic poet

10. Who are the four musical masters of the Viennese school?

    a. _____   b. _____

    c. _____   d. _____

11. Check those characteristics below that properly describe the Classical musical style (one check per grouping).

_____ a. disjunct, wide-ranging melodies *or*

_____ b. simple, singable melodies

_____ c. regular, symmetrical phrasing with clear cadences *or*

_____ d. irregular, asymmetrical phrasing with weak or covered cadences

_____ e. chromatic harmony *or*

_____ f. diatonic harmony

_____ g. free, programmatic forms *or*

_____ h. large-scale, absolute forms

_____ i. incorporation of folk songs and dances *or*

_____ j. incorporation of non-Western melodies

_____ k. weak or free meters *or*

_____ l. strong, regular meters

12. How would you describe the patronage system? What were the advantages and disadvantages to artists serving under this system?

_____

_____

_____

_____

_____

13. What role did women play in music during this era?

_____

_____

_____

_____

39. *Explore* Concert Life in the Americas: Then and Now
CP 8 Chr/Sh; 7 Std

Exercises

Complete the following questions.

1. Which composers were heard most frequently in North American concerts of the eighteenth century? _____

   _____

2. Describe some aspects of eighteenth-century concerts in North America.

   _____

   _____

   _____

   _____

3. How did opera performances differ from those today?

   _____

   _____

4. What was the first opera written in North America? _____
   Who wrote it and where was it premiered? _____

5. What is the literal meaning of the word "encore"? _____
   What does it mean when the audience asks for an encore?

   _____

6. Which famous American statesmen were amateur musicians?

   _____

7. What musical abilities were considered desirable for eighteenth-century women? _____

   _____

   _____

8. Name several major music organizations that first appeared in the nineteenth century. _____

   _____

Library Assignment

Go to the microfilm section of your college (or community) library. Investigate whether they have any eighteenth- or nineteenth-century newspapers on film there (for example, the *New York Times* or the *Boston Globe*). If available, select a film from this era at random, put it on the machine (following the directions for threading the film), and scroll through until you find an announcement of an upcoming concert. Answer the questions below.

Or locate a concert announcement in the calendar section of a current newspaper. Note the following information.

Title of newspaper: _____

Date of issue consulted: _____

Section and page of announcement: _____

Concert information (date, time, price, location):

_____

_____

_____

List the works and composers to be performed.

_____

_____

_____

Or visit the Web site (www.wwnorton.com/enjoy), read the Cultural Perspective, and describe below the path you chose through the Web links.

_____

_____

_____

_____

_____

_____

_____

_____

> **40. *Review* Chamber Music and Symphony in the Classical Era**
> **Chaps.** 31–33 Chr/Sh; 43–45 Std

Exercises

CHAMBER MUSIC

Answer the following questions.

1. What is chamber music? _____

2. What was the favored chamber ensemble in the Classical era, and what
   is its makeup? _____

   _____

3. Name several other common chamber ensembles. _____

   _____

4. Name several forms of popular-entertainment music during the era.

   _____

Match each of the following string quartet movements with the form it
would most likely take.

_____ 5. first movement   a. theme and variations form

_____ 6. second movement   b. rondo form

_____ 7. third movement   c. sonata-allegro form

_____ 8. fourth movement   d. minuet and trio form

Match the following string quartet traits with the composer best associated
with each.

_____ 9. use of folk elements   a. Mozart

_____ 10. scherzo replacing minuet   b. Haydn

_____ 11. motivic development   c. Beethoven

_____ 12. lyrical, elegant themes

THE SYMPHONY

13. From which earlier form did the symphony evolve? _____

14. What contributions did Mannheim musicians make to the symphony?

   _____

79

15. Approximately how many players made up a Classical-era orchestra? _____ Which instrument families are represented?_____

_____

16. In what type of setting were symphonies performed in the eighteenth century? _____

In what setting are they performed today? _____

17. Which movement of the symphony is generally the longest and the most complex? _____

What is its form? _____

18. Which movement is generally the fastest? _____

What are typical forms for this movement? _____

_____

19. Which movement is based on a dance form? _____

What is the character of this dance movement?_____

_____

20. Which movement is generally the slowest? _____

What forms are typical for it? _____

_____

21. Which movement is probably the most lyrical? _____

22. What does the term "monothematic" mean relating to the symphony?

_____

Which composer is associated with this form?

_____

> ## 41. *Listen* Eighteenth-Century Chamber Music
> *Haydn: String Quartet Op. 76, No. 2, Fourth Movement (**LG** 29 Chr; 22 Std; *e***LG**)
>
> Mozart: *Eine kleine Nachtmusik*, K. 525 (**LG** 30 Chr; 15 Sh; 23 Std; *e***LG**)

Exercises

*Listen to the last movement of Haydn's Quartet, Op. 76, No. 2, while following the Listening Guide, then answer questions 1–8.

   1. How many string quartets did Haydn write? _____

   2. When were his Opus 76 quartets written? _____

   3. In which key is Op. 76, No. 2 written? _____

   4. How many movements does this quartet have? _____

   5. Give the general tempo and form for each movement.

      I. _____

      II. _____

     III. _____

     IV. _____

   6. What is the nickname for this quartet? _____

     Why is it called this? _____

   7. What elements make the fourth movement sound dance-like?

     _____

     _____

   8. Describe the sound of the Classical-period string instruments on this

     recording. _____

     _____

Listen to Mozart's *Eine kleine Nachtmusik* while following the Listening Guide, then answer questions 9–18.

   9. What does the title *Eine kleine Nachtmusik* mean literally?

     _____

  10. Is this work _____ a string quartet or _____ a serenade?

     What size ensemble was it written for? _____

11. List the general tempo and form for each movement.

I. _____

II. _____

III. _____

IV. _____

12. In what key is the work? _____

Which movement is not in this key? _____

13. How would you describe the themes in the first movement?

1st theme: _____

2nd theme: _____

14. How would you describe the mood of the second movement?

_____

15. Listen for the short, repeated parts within the first sections. Can you hear

the repeats? _____ Are the phrases balanced (symmetrical)? _____

16. How would you describe the themes in the third movement?

Minuet: _____

Trio: _____

Which section sounds more dance-like? _____

17. How does Mozart create contrast with the two themes of the last

movement? _____

_____

18. For what kind of concert setting was this piece written?

_____

_____

---

42. *Listen* The Eighteenth-Century Symphony

*Mozart: Symphony No. 40, First Movement (**LG** 31 Chr; 24 Std; *e***LG**)
Haydn: Symphony No. 94, Second Movement (**LG** 32 Chr; 16 Sh; 25 Std; *e***LG**)
Beethoven: Symphony No. 5 (**LG** 33 Chr; 17 Sh; 26 Std; *e***LG**)

Exercises

*Listen to Mozart's Symphony No. 40 in G minor while following the Listening Guide, then answer questions 1–5.

1. What is the overall form of this symphony (movements and tempo)?

   _____

   _____

2. Describe the motive that provides the building block for the first theme.

   _____

3. What techniques does Mozart use to vary material in the development section of the first movement?

   _____

   _____

4. Unlike many Classical-era symphonies, Mozart's Symphony No. 40 is in the minor mode. What effect is produced by this choice of harmony?

   _____

   _____

5. Why was this symphony called the "Romantic" by the Viennese?

   _____

   _____

Listen to Haydn's Symphony No. 94, second movement, and Beethoven's Symphony No. 5 while following the Listening Guides, then answer questions 6–13.

6. Complete the following chart.

	SYMPHONY NO. 94	SYMPHONY NO. 5
a. First movement		
Tempo:	_____	_____
Form:	_____	_____

b. Second movement

Tempo: _____ _____

Form: _____ _____

c. Third movement

Tempo: _____ _____

Form: _____ _____

d. Fourth movement

Tempo: _____ _____

Form: _____ _____

7. Do both symphonies follow the standard multimovement cycle plan?

_____

8. How does Haydn "surprise" his listeners in the second movement of

Symphony No. 94? _____

_____

9. Describe the timbres of the Classical-period instruments heard on this
recording.

Strings _____

Bass _____

Woodwinds _____

10. What are the differences in size and instrumentation between Haydn's

orchestra and Beethoven's? _____

_____

11. What makes the first movement of Beethoven's Symphony No. 5 so

memorable? _____

_____

11. What traits of the Beethoven symphony sound Romantic?

_____

_____

12. What are some of the innovations that Beethoven introduced in this

symphony? _____

_____

_____

_____

43. *Review* The Classical Masters
Chaps. 32, 34–35 Chr/Sh; 44, 46–47 Std

Exercises

For each of the following, choose the composer who best fits the description below.

> a. Joseph Haydn
> b. Wolfgang Amadeus Mozart
> c. Ludwig van Beethoven

_____ 1. The composer who was a child prodigy as a composer and performer.

_____ 2. The composer who grew deaf at the height of his compositional career.

_____ 3. The composer generally known as the "father of the symphony."

_____ 4. The composer who died young, while writing a Requiem Mass.

_____ 5. The composer who thrived for many years under the patronage system.

_____ 6. The composer of the "London" symphonies.

_____ 7. The composer of thirty-two piano sonatas, including the *Moonlight*.

_____ 8. The composer who is well-known for opera buffa.

_____ 9. The composer whose last symphony includes a choral setting of Schiller's *Ode to Joy*.

_____ 10. The composer who spanned the transition between the Classical and Romantic eras.

11. List for comparison the number of symphonies written by each composer below.

    Haydn _____   Mozart _____   Beethoven _____

12. Why did Mozart write fewer symphonies than Haydn?

    _____

    _____

13. Why did Beethoven write fewer symphonies than Haydn or Mozart?

    _____

    _____

14. What European country can be associated with the lives of all three of these musicians? _____

Multiple Choice

____ 15. The K. number following each Mozart work refers to the:
   a. name of the man who catalogued his compositions.
   b. key, or tonality, of the composition.

____ 16. Which Mozart opera was written in German and was popular in the Viennese theater?
   a. *The Magic Flute*
   b. *The Marriage of Figaro*

____ 17. Haydn worked for many years for the:
   a. Prince-Archbishop of Salzburg.
   b. Hungarian noble family of Esterházy.

____ 18. Which was a popular oratorio by Haydn?
   a. *The Creation*
   b. *Messiah*

____ 19. Which composer wrote only one opera, *Fidelio?*
   a. Joseph Haydn
   b. Ludwig van Beethoven

____ 20. Late in his life, Haydn made several visits to _____, where he was commissioned to write a group of symphonies.
   a. Italy
   b. England

____ 21. The composer of the *Eroica* Symphony was:
   a. Beethoven.
   b. Mozart.

22. How do you account for the continued popularity of these three Classical composers?

_____

_____

_____

_____

_____

44. *Explore* The Composer Heard 'round the World
CP 9 Chr/Sh; 8 Std   [e]

Exercises

Answer the following questions.

1. What was the public reaction to Beethoven's Symphony No. 5 at its premiere? _____

   _____

   _____

   Was this a typical reaction to "new music"? _____

2. Describe how Beethoven came to be known throughout the Western world during his lifetime. _____

   _____

   _____

3. What Beethoven work was performed at the first concert given by the New York Philharmonic? _____

4. Describe the famous opening motive of Beethoven's Symphony No. 5.

   _____

5. Why was this motive important during World War II?

   _____

   _____

6. Who wrote the text that Beethoven set in the finale to his Symphony No. 9? _____

7. What is this text popularly called? _____

8. How does Beethoven figure in New Year's traditions in Japan?

   _____

   _____

9. What popular arrangements have been made of Beethoven's symphonies?

   _____

   _____

Listening Assignment

Locate a recording (or video) of Beethoven's Symphony No. 9. Listen to the finale (the fourth movement), read the text, then describe the work below.

Or read the Cultural Perspective on the Web site (www.wwnorton.com/enjoy), explore the Web links, and answer the questions below.

What is the text of this movement about? _____

_____

_____

Describe the vocal melody sung by the soloists and chorus.

_____

_____

Describe the march (about eight minutes into the movement). Consider the meter and instruments used.

_____

_____

_____

_____

_____

_____

What other musical elements help to deliver the message of the text?

_____

_____

_____

_____

_____

Why do you think this work has been popular the world over?

_____

_____

_____

_____

---

45. *Review* The Concerto and Sonata in the Classical Era
Chaps. 36–37 Chr/Sh; 48–49 Std

Exercises

Multiple Choice

_____ 1. How many movements are standard in a concerto?
    a. two   c. four
    b. three   d. five or more

_____ 2. How many movements are standard in a sonata?
    a. one or two   c. three or four
    b. two or three   d. five or more

_____ 3. Which tempo scheme is standard for the concerto?
    a. slow–fast   c. fast–slow–fast
    b. fast–slow–fast–faster   d. slow–moderate–fast

4. What is a cadenza, and when is it usually played? _____

_____

_____

5. What two forms does the first movement of a concerto adapt?

_____

6. What were the favored solo instruments in the Classical concerto?

_____

7. What instrument(s) did Mozart play?

_____

8. For whom did he write his Piano Concerto in G major, K. 453?

_____

9. What were the favored instruments in the Classical sonata?

_____

10. What is a duo sonata? _____

_____

Match the following virtuoso performers with the correct description.

a. Barbara von Ployer   c. Maria Anna Mozart
b. Maddalena Lombardini   d. Maria Theresa von Paradis

____ 11. An accomplished pianist who was Mozart's sister.

____ 12. A gifted piano student of Mozart's, for whom he wrote two concertos.

____ 13. A talented blind pianist and organist, for whom both Mozart and Salieri wrote concertos.

____ 14. A virtuoso violinist who was a student of Tartini and also a composer of violin concertos.

15. Choose two of the women above, and describe how each excelled as a musician.

a. _____

_____

_____

_____

b. _____

_____

_____

_____

46. *Explore* East Meets West: Turkish Influences on the Viennese Classics
CP 10 Chr/Sh; 9 Std

Exercises

Answer the following questions.

1. To which empire did eighteenth-century Austria belong?

_____

To which empire did Turkey belong? _____

2. What is a Janissary band? _____

_____

When and where did it originate?

_____

3. How did Western Europeans come to know the sound of the Janissary ensemble? _____

_____

4. What instruments were added to this band in the seventeenth century?

_____

_____

5. Which Classical composers tried to imitate the Janissary band in their music? _____

6. What permanent contribution did this ensemble make to the Western orchestra? _____

_____

7. What other Western music group did the Janissary ensemble influence?

_____

8. Which Islamic religious ceremony did Beethoven attempt to imitate in *The Ruins of Athens*? _____

Describe this ceremony. _____

_____

_____

Listening Assignment

Locate a recording of Turkish music in your library (or ask your instructor to provide one from the Music Example Bank). Listen to it and describe the musical style and instruments in your own words. Note what sounds foreign about it and what sounds familiar.

Or visit the Web site (www.wwnorton.com/enjoy), read the Cultural Perspective, then describe below the path you chose through the Web links.

_____

_____

_____

_____

_____

_____

_____

_____

_____

_____

_____

_____

_____

_____

_____

_____

_____

_____

_____

_____

_____

_____

_____

_____

_____

_____

---

47. *Listen* The Classical Concerto and Sonata

Mozart: Piano Concerto in G major, K. 453, First Movement; *Second and
*Third Movements (**LG** 34 Chr; 18 Sh; 27 Std; *e***LG**)

*Beethoven: Violin Concerto in D major, Op. 61, Third Movement (**LG** 35 Chr;
28 Std; *e***LG**)

Beethoven: Piano Sonata in C minor, Op. 13 (*Pathétique*) (**LG** 37 Chr; 19 Sh;
30 Std; *e***LG**)

*Mozart: Piano Sonata in A major, K. 331, Third Movement (**LG** 36 Chr;
29 Std; *e***LG**)

Exercises

*Listen to the Mozart piano concerto while following the Listening Guide,
then answer questions 1–6.

1. Describe the character of the themes as stated by the orchestra in the
   first movement.

   Theme 1: _____

   Theme 2: _____

2. Describe the first theme as heard in the solo exposition with piano.

   _____

   _____

3. How many times and where do you hear the "piano theme"?

   _____

   _____

4. What is a cadenza? _____

   What themes do you recognize in the first-movement cadenza?

   _____

*5. How would you describe the mood of the second movement?

   _____

*6. In the third movement, describe each variation of the theme.

   Variation 1: _____

   Variation 2: _____

   Variation 3: _____

   Variation 4: _____

   Variation 5: _____

*Listen to the third movement of Beethoven's Violin Concerto while following the Listening Guide, then answer questions 7–8.

7. Describe the character of the main violin theme. _____

_____

8. What is the form of the movement? _____

In how many sections does it occur? _____

Listen to Beethoven's *Pathétique* Sonata, then answer questions 9–11.

9. How did this piano sonata get the name *Pathétique?*

_____

_____

10. What could be viewed as "Romantic" about the *Pathétique* sonata?

_____

_____

11. What is the form and tempo of each movement?

　　I. _____

　　II. _____

　　III. _____

*Listen to Mozart's Piano Sonata in A major, third movement, then answer questions 12–14.

12. What is the form of this movement? _____

What is the meter? _____

13. Why is it subtitled "alla turca"? What are the special effects heard in this movement?

_____

_____

14. Of the works studied, the Mozart concerto and sonata, and the Beethoven sonata feature the piano as a solo instrument. How do you account for the popularity of the piano in the eighteenth century?

_____

_____

_____

_____

48. *Listen* Haydn and Classical Choral Music
*Haydn: *The Creation*, Part I, Nos. 12–14 (**LG** 38 Chr; 31 Std; *e***LG**)

Exercises
Answer the following questions on choral forms.

1. What is the difference between a Mass and a Requiem Mass?

   _____

   _____

2. Which Classical composer wrote a famous Requiem Mass?

   _____

3. Name two well-known oratorios by Haydn.

   _____ and _____

*Listen to the excerpts from Haydn's *The Creation* while following the Listening Guide, then answer questions 4–13.

4. What were the literary sources for the text of *The Creation*?

   _____

   _____

5. Which biblical characters are featured in the oratorio?

   _____

   _____

6. How does Haydn achieve a memorable effect on the words "Let there be light"?

   _____

7. How was the first performance of the oratorio received by critics?

   _____

8. There are two types of recitative heard in our excerpt. Describe how each sounds, and give a line of text where each style is heard.

   secco: _____

   text: _____

   accompagnato: _____

   text: _____

9. Which day of creation does Uriel's recitative describe? _____

    According to the text, what was created on that day? _____

    _____

10. How would you describe the texture of the opening of the chorus (on

    the text "The Heavens are telling")? _____

11. At which point in the text do you hear the soloists singing in imitation

    (overlapping entries)? _____

12. Describe in your own words the mood of this chorus.

    _____

    _____

    _____

13. Would a modern choral work on this text and subject be effective

    today? _____ Why or why not? _____

    _____

    _____

    _____

> ## 49. *Listen* Mozart's *The Marriage of Figaro*
> Mozart: *The Marriage of Figaro,* *Overture and Act I, Scenes 6 and 7 (**LG** 39 Chr;
> 20 Sh; 32 Std; *e***LG**)

Exercises

Listen to the selections on your recording from *The Marriage of Figaro* while
following the Listening Guide, then answer the questions below.

1. What type (genre) of opera is this? _____

2. What are some of the typical characteristics of this opera type?

   _____

   _____

3. How does this opera differ from opera seria? _____

   _____

   _____

4. Who was the librettist for *The Marriage of Figaro?*

   _____

5. Name several Mozart operas by the same librettist.

   _____

6. What was the literary basis for *The Marriage of Figaro?*

   _____

7. In what ways does this opera satirize the aristocracy?

   _____

   _____

8. What is a trouser role? _____

   _____

9. Is the trouser role convincing in *The Marriage of Figaro?*

   _____

10. What do you learn about the character of Cherubino from the aria

    (No. 6)? _____

    _____

11. What purpose is served by the long recitative between Cherubino's aria and the trio in *The Marriage of Figaro?*

_____

_____

_____

12. Consider the three characters singing in the trio (No. 7), and suggest below what emotion each is expressing and how the music helps communicate this emotion.

The Count: _____

_____

Basilio: _____

_____

Susanna: _____

_____

13. What aspects of the plot of *The Marriage of Figaro* strike you as unrealistic or far-fetched?

_____

_____

_____

14. In what ways would this story be changed in a modern-day update?

_____

_____

_____

50. *Review* Schubert and the Transition from Classicism to Romanticism
Trans. III Chr/Sh; I Std

Exercises

Answer the following questions.

1. Which Classical master's music foreshadowed the Romantic style?

   _____

2. What are some of the Romantic characteristics in his music?

   _____

   _____

3. Which early Romantic composer can be viewed as the direct heir of the

   Classical tradition?

   _____

4. In which genres is this composer considered Classical?

   _____

   In which genres is he more Romantic in style? _____

5. What is a Lied? _____

6. What Romantic fascination does the song *The Trout* represent?

   _____

7. What chamber work did Schubert base on his song *The Trout?*

   _____

COMPARING CLASSICAL AND ROMANTIC STYLES

8. Name the three great Classical masters.

   _____

9. Name at least three Romantic composers.

   _____

   _____

For each of the following musical traits, indicate whether it is best associated with the Classical or the Romantic style.

      a. Classical style
      b. Romantic style

_____ 10. interest in the bizarre and macabre

_____ 11. diatonic harmony predominant

_____ 12. use of unusual ranges of instruments

_____ 13. use of one-movement programmatic forms

_____ 14. dance rhythms with regular beats and accents

_____ 15. rise of a middle-class audience

_____ 16. use of freer rhythms and tempo rubato

_____ 17. emotional restraint

_____ 18. symmetrical, balanced phrases

_____ 19. wide-ranging dynamic contrasts

_____ 20. introduction of the English horn and tuba

_____ 21. preference for absolute forms

_____ 22. sonata-allegro form established

_____ 23. aristocratic audiences

_____ 24. much expanded melodic and harmonic chromaticism

25. What are the approximate dates of the Classical period?

_____ the Romantic period? _____

26. Do you think the arts today lean more toward Romantic or Classical traits? _____ Explain your answer.

_____

_____

_____

_____

_____

> ## 51. *Listen* Schubert: From Song to Chamber Music
> *Schubert: *The Trout* and *Trout* Quintet, Fourth Movement (**LG** 40 Chr; 33 Std; *e***LG**)

Exercises

*Listen to the two works listed above while following the Listening Guide, then answer the questions below.

   1. Who wrote the poem *The Trout?* _____

   2. What is the poem's form? _____

   3. What is the German title of this poem? _____

   4. Describe the story told in the poem. _____

     _____

   5. What is the musical form of Schubert's song *The Trout?*

     _____

   6. How and where is the music modified? _____

     _____

   7. What role does the piano play in telling the story? _____

     _____

   8. What is folk-like about this song? _____

     _____

   9. For which movement of his Piano Quintet did Schubert use this song?

     _____

  10. What is the instrumentation of the Piano Quintet?

     _____

  11. What is unusual about this instrumentation? _____

     _____

  12. How many movements does this quintet have? _____

     Is this number typical? _____

  13. What is the form of the fourth movement? _____

14. The main theme is heard in two parts, with each repeated. Which is longer? _____

15. For each variation, note which instrument(s) has(have) the main melody.

    Variation 1: _____

    Variation 2: _____

    Variation 3: _____

    Variation 4: _____

    Variation 5: _____

    Variation 6: _____

16. In which variation does the harmony shift to a minor key?

    _____

    How does this shift affect the mood?

    _____

17. Does this quintet seem Classical or Romantic in style? Explain.

    _____

    _____

    _____

---

52. *Review* The Romantic Movement
Chaps. 40–41 Chr; 39–40 Sh; 11–12 Std

Exercises

Answer the following questions.

1. What were the ideals of the early Romantic movement?

   _____

   _____

2. What social changes resulted from the French Revolution?

   _____

   _____

3. What was the slogan of the revolution? _____

Match the following Romantic figures with the descriptions on the right.

_____ 4. Heinrich Heine   a. English novelist

_____ 5. Victor Hugo   b. French painter

_____ 6. Eugène Delacroix   c. German poet

_____ 7. Nathaniel Hawthorne   d. American writer

_____ 8. Emily Brontë   e. French novelist

9. What effect did the Industrial Revolution have on the production of

   musical instruments? _____

   _____

   _____

   _____

10. What new instruments were developed in the Romantic era?

    _____

    _____

    _____

11. Which sections of the orchestra grew substantially during the Romantic
    era?

    _____

    _____

12. How were educational opportunities in music affected during the era?

_____

_____

13. What is meant by "exoticism" in music? _____

_____

_____

14. Name a musical work that is representative of exoticism.

Composer: _____ Title: _____

Multiple Choice

____ 15. Which of the following is NOT typical of Romantic music?
a. lyrical, singable melodies
b. expanded forms
c. smaller orchestras
d. increased dissonance for expression

____ 16. Which role did Romantic composers generally NOT fill?
a. educators
b. servants to the aristocracy
c. performing artists
d. conductors

Complete the following questions.

17. Who were the musical "stars" in the nineteenth century?

_____

_____

18. What roles in music did women fill in the Romantic era?

_____

_____

19. What educational opportunities in music were open to women?

_____

_____

20. What prejudices did women musicians, artists, and writers have to contend with in the nineteenth century?

_____

_____

_____

_____

---

53. *Review* The Nineteenth-Century Art Song
Chaps. 42–45 Chr; 41–43 Sh; 13–16 Std

Exercises

Complete the following questions.

1. A song form in which the same melody is repeated for each stanza, often heard in popular music, is known as _____.

2. A song form that is composed from beginning to end without repetitions of whole sections is called _____.

3. A song type that features some repetition or variations of a melody and new material is known as _____.

4. A group of Lieder unified by a descriptive or narrative theme is known as a _____. Name one and its composer.

   _____

True or False

____ 5. A Lied is a German art song for solo voice and piano.

____ 6. Folk elements are sometimes incorporated into the Lied.

____ 7. The composer normally writes the lyrics for the Lied.

____ 8. The Lied composer often attempts to portray musically the imagery of the poem.

____ 9. The favorite themes of the Lied include love and nature.

____ 10. The piano was declining in popularity at the time of the Romantic Lied.

11. Name one important German poet whose texts were frequently set to music; list one specific work and its composer.

   POET   POEM   COMPOSER

   _____   _____   _____

12. Name two additional important composers of Lieder.

   a. _____

   b. _____

13. When was Schubert's *Erlking* written? _____

    How old was the composer when he wrote it?_____

    Who wrote the poem? _____

14. What is Schubert's *Winter's Journey*? _____

15. Approximately how many songs did Schubert write? _____

*16. What is a "Schubertiad"? _____

SCHUMANN AS A LIED COMPOSER

17. About how many songs did Robert Schumann write? _____

18. What is the most common theme in Schumann's songs?

    _____

19. Name two song cycles by Robert Schumann.

    _____

20. On whose texts is Schumann's *A Poet's Love* set? _____

*FANNY MENDELSSOHN HENSEL AND ROMANTIC SONG

21. Approximately how many songs did Fanny Mendelssohn Hensel write?

    _____

22. Who were her favorite poets? _____

23. Her last composition, written just days before her death, was a song.

    What was its title? _____

24. What is the general subject of the song? _____

25. Why did women write in small-scale genres, such as the Lied, more

    often than in larger symphonic forms? _____

    _____

---

54. *Listen* **Romantic Lieder**

Schubert: *Erlking* (**LG** 41 Chr; 21 Sh; 2 Std; *e***LG**)

Schumann: "And if the flowers knew,: from *A Poet's Love* (**LG** 42 Chr; 22 Sh; 3 Std; *e***LG**)

*Fanny Mendelssohn Hensel: *Mountain Yearning*, Op. 10, No. 5 (**LG** 43 Chr; 4 Std; *e***LG**)

Exercises

Listen to Schubert's *Erlking* while following the Listening Guide, then answer questions 1–5.

1. How does the piano establish the mood of Schubert's *Erlking* at the beginning of the song? _____

_____

2. What is the form of this song? _____

Is any music or idea repeated? _____

3. Describe how Schubert portrays each of the four characters in the song musically with only one singer.

Narrator: _____

Father: _____

Son: _____

Erlking: _____

4. How does Schubert use dissonance for dramatic effect?

_____

5. Bearing in mind the drama of Schubert's *Erlking,* suggest a story (either from literature or from a movie) that you think would make a successful Lied, with solo voice and piano. Briefly describe the story and suggest some effects that might be achieved in the Lied.

_____

_____

_____

_____

_____

_____

Listen to the Robert Schumann song "And if the flowers knew," from *A Poet's Love* while following the Listening Guide, then answer questions 6–11.

6. What is the form of this song? _____

7. How would you describe the character of the melody?

_____

8. What is the text about? _____

_____

9. How does the tone of the poem change in the last strophe?

_____

10. How does Schumann change the music for this last strophe?

_____

_____

11. Describe the role of the piano in this song. _____

_____

*Listen to Fanny Mendelssohn Hensel's *Mountain Yearning* while following the Listening Guide, then answer questions 12–16.

12. What is the poetic form of this text? _____

13. What is the musical form of the Lied? _____

14. What makes this song seem folk-like? _____

_____

15. Cite an example of text painting from this Lied.

_____

16. Describe how the piano contributes to the mood of this song.

_____

> ## 55. *Review* The Nineteenth-Century Piano Piece and Its Composers
> **Chaps.** 46–49 Chr; 44–46 Sh; 17–20 Std

Exercises

True or False

_____ 1. The piano became a popular instrument for amateur musicians.

_____ 2. The piano changed little technically during the nineteenth century.

_____ 3. The nineteenth century was an age of great virtuoso pianists.

4. Which nineteenth-century composers contributed to modern piano technique? _____

5. What are some of the descriptive titles that Romantic composers gave to their piano works? _____

_____

6. Why is Chopin called the "poet of the piano"?

_____

_____

7. What was Chopin's national heritage? _____

8. What is tempo rubato? _____

9. With which famous writer was Chopin romantically involved?

_____

10. In which small forms of piano music did Chopin write?

_____

In which large forms did he write? _____

Of these forms, which can be viewed as nationalistic?

_____

11. What music did Chopin write that did NOT include piano?

_____

*12. In which country was Franz Liszt born? _____

*13. With which famous writer was Liszt romantically involved?

_____

109

*14. What other aristocratic woman was important in Liszt's life?

_____

*15. What lifestyle did Liszt choose in his later years?

_____

*16. Liszt devised a technique of developing a theme through constant
variation of its melody, rhythm, or harmony. This process is known
as _____.

*17. Which composer did Liszt describe as writing the "music of the future"?

_____

18. Describe Clara Schumann's early musical training.

_____

19. In which musical genres did Clara Schumann write? _____

_____

20. What was her relationship with Robert Schumann? _____
with Brahms? _____

21. What was the public reaction to Clara Schumann as a pianist?

_____

22. What difficulties did a woman composer have in the nineteenth century?

_____

_____

_____

_____

---

56. *Listen* **Romantic Piano Music**
   Chopin: Nocturne in C minor, Op. 48, No. 1 (**LG** 44 Chr; 23 Sh; 5 Std; *e***LG**)
   *Chopin: Prelude in E minor, Op. 28, No. 4 (**LG** 45 Chr; 6 Std; *e***LG**)
   *Liszt: *La campanella* (*The Little Bell*) (**LG** 46 Chr; 7 Std; *e***LG**)
   Clara Schumann: Scherzo, Op. 10 (**LG** 47 Chr; 24 Sh; 8 Std; *e***LG**)

Exercises

Listen to Chopin's Nocturne in C minor while following the Listening Guide, then answer questions 1–4.

1. What is the general character of a nocturne? _____

   _____

2. How is the Nocturne in C minor different from others that Chopin

   wrote? _____

3. Describe the mood of the contrasting middle section (**B**) of the work.

   _____

4. Does the performance you heard use tempo rubato? _____

   Where in the piece? _____

*Listen to Chopin's Prelude in E minor while following the Listening Guide, then answer questions 5–10 (check one).

5. This prelude is a:

   ___ a. large-scale, multisectional work for piano.

   ___ b. small character work for piano.

6. The opening phrase of this prelude is:

   ___ a. disjunct with a wide range.

   ___ b. conjunct with a narrow range.

7. The work is performed with:

   ___ a. some freedom or rubato in the rhythm.

   ___ b. strict tempo and rhythm.

8. The meter is:

   ___ a. strong and dancelike in this work.

   ___ b. gentle and veiled in this work.

9. How would you characterize the mood of this work?

   _____

10. Do you think this prelude is difficult to perform well? _____

   Explain. _____

*Listen to Liszt's *La campanella* while following the Listening Guide, then
   answer questions 11–14.

11. To which collection does *The Little Bell* belong? _____

   What is the purpose of these works? _____

   _____

12. On whose composition is this work based? _____

13. How does Liszt evoke the sound of a bell in this work?

   _____

   _____

   _____

14. What makes this work virtuosic (or very difficult to play)?

   _____

   _____

Listen to Clara Schumann's Scherzo, Op. 10, while following the Listening
Guide, then answer questions 15–18.

15. Describe the character of each section of this work.

   Scherzo theme: _____

   Trio 1: _____

   Trio 2: _____

16. Does the marking *con passione* (with passion) seem appropriate? _____

   Explain. _____

   _____

17. What are some of the features that make this a display work?

   _____

   _____

18. In your opinion, is there anything about this work that seems
   "feminine"? _____ Explain. _____

   _____

---

57. *Review* Romantic Program Music and Nationalism
Chaps. 50–52 Chr; 47–49 Sh; 21–23 Std

Exercises

Match the following terms with their definitions.

    a. absolute music   d. program music
    b. concert overture   e. incidental music
    c. program symphony   f. symphonic poem

_____ 1. Instrumental music that has some literary or pictorial association supplied by the composer.

_____ 2. Music lacking any literary or pictorial association.

_____ 3. A type of program music written to accompany plays.

_____ 4. A one-movement work for orchestra with a literary program.

_____ 5. A multi-movement orchestral work with literary program.

_____ 6. A one-movement work originally written to introduce a larger work, but played independently.

Multiple Choice

_____ 7. Which composer is generally credited with the first use of the term "symphonic poem"?
    a. Franz Liszt
    b. Hector Berlioz
    c. Felix Mendelssohn

_____ 8. The chief difference between a symphonic poem and a program symphony is the:
    a. nature of the program.
    b. number of movements in the work.
    c. number of musicians involved.

9. Name a famous example of incidental music.

_____

10. What example of a program symphony did we study? _____

_____

11. In what ways do composers express their nationalism through music?

_____

_____

Match the following composers with the correct national school.

    a. Russian school   d. English school
    b. Czech school   e. Spanish school
    c. Scandinavian school

____ 12. Jean Sibelius   ___ 16. Edvard Grieg

____ 13. Bedřich Smetana   ___ 17. Alexander Borodin

____ 14. Manuel de Falla   ___ 18. Edward Elgar

____ 15. Peter Ilyich Tchaikovsky ___ 19. Antonín Dvořák

20. The term "program music" can apply to music for film and television as well as to nineteenth-century instrumental music. Briefly describe a movie or television production you have seen recently and tell how the music helped to portray the story or establish the mood.

Program: _____

_____

_____

_____

_____

_____

Musical description: _____

_____

_____

_____

_____

_____

_____

---

58. *Listen* Berlioz and Smetana
Berlioz: *Symphonie fantastique,* Fourth and *Fifth Movements (**LG** 48 Chr; 25 Sh; 9 Std; *e***LG**)
Smetana: *The Moldau* (**LG** 49 Chr; 26 Sh; 10 Std; *e***LG**)

Exercises

Listen to Berlioz's *Symphonie fantastique* while following the Listening Guide, then answer questions 1–9.

1. When and where did Berlioz write the *Symphonie fantastique?*

   _____

2. What is "Romantic" about this work and its program?

   _____

   _____

   _____

3. Who was the inspiration behind this work?

   _____

4. What is an *idée fixe* in music? _____

   _____

5. How does Berlioz use this technique to unify his symphony?

   _____

6. What is the mood of the March (fourth movement)?

   _____

7. Can you hear the graphic musical "decapitation"? _____

   What effect does it have? _____

*8. What effect does the use of the *Dies irae* chant have in the last

   movement? _____

9. Do you perceive any differences between the sounds of Romantic-

   period instruments (heard in the Berlioz *Symphonie fantastique*) and

   modern instruments (in other recordings)? _____

   Explain. _____

   _____

   _____

Listen to Smetana's *The Moldau* while following the Listening Guide, then answer questions 10–14.

_____ 10. Which type of program best describes *The Moldau?*
      a. literary, based on a play or novel
      b. philosophical, based on a conceptual idea
      c. graphic, depicting actual events or places

_____ 11. Which category of program music best describes *The Moldau?*
      a. program symphony
      b. symphonic poem
      c. incidental music

12. Which instruments does Smetana use to evoke the following?

    a. two streams joining: _____

    b. a flowing river: _____

    c. a hunting scene: _____

    d. moonlight on the water: _____

    e. memories of an ancient castle: _____

13. What circumstances might inspire a composer or artist to produce a nationalistic work?

_____

_____

_____

14. Suggest an event or place that might inspire a modern-day nationalist composer.

_____

_____

_____

_____

59. *Explore* Music and Nationalism
CP 11 Chr/Sh; 3 Std

Exercises

Complete the following questions.

1. What lessons do folktales teach?_____

_____

_____

2. Cite a folktale you know and its moral or lesson.

_____

_____

_____

_____

3. Who is the Russian folk figure Baba-Yaga? _____

_____

_____

4. From which folk collection does the tale of "Hansel and Gretel" come?

_____

5. What is the source of the tale of "Aladdin"? _____

_____

Of "Sleeping Beauty" and "Cinderella"? _____

_____

Of "The Little Mermaid"? _____

6. What is the folk basis for Tchaikovsky's well-known ballet *The Nutcracker*?

_____

_____

7. What musical genres lend themselves to settings of folktales?

_____

Listening Assignment

Listen to one of the musical works below that sets a folktale. Familiarize yourself with the story (find the original tale or read over the recording notes) and describe below how the music portrays the events of the story.

Maurice Ravel, from *Mother Goose Suite* (*Ma mère l'oye*) (French tales by Perrault), one of the following movements: *Pavane de la Belle au bois dormant* (*Sleeping Beauty*) or *Petit Poucet* (*Tom Thumb*)

Sergei Prokofiev, *Cinderella* (ballet suite after Perrault tale)

Peter Ilyich Tchaikovsky, *The Sleeping Beauty*, Op. 66a (ballet suite after Perrault tale)

Richard Strauss, *Till Eulenspiegel's Merry Pranks* (German tale)

Sergei Prokofiev, *Peter and the Wolf* (modern Russian tale)

Or visit the Web site (www.wwnorton.com/enjoy), read the Cultural Perspective, and describe below the path you chose through the Web links.

_____

_____

_____

_____

_____

_____

_____

_____

_____

_____

_____

_____

_____

_____

_____

_____

_____

_____

_____

_____

_____

> **60.** *Review* **Absolute Forms: The Symphony and the Concerto**
> **Chaps.** 53, 56 Chr; 50, 52 Sh; 24, 27 Std

Terms to Remember

absolute music   scherzo
cadenza   sonata-allegro form
concerto   symphony
motive   theme
                                        tutti

Exercises

Complete the following questions.

1. The symphony is a large-scale work for orchestra, made up of several

   independent parts, or _____.

2. The symphony first became an important form in the _____

   era.

3. Three composers in Vienna who mastered the form and handed it

   down to Romantic composers were _____,

   _____, and _____.

4. The symphony cycle most typically has _____ movements.

5. Of these, the _____ movement is usually the most highly

   structured, and features the use of _____ form.

6. What forms are typical for the second movement of a symphony?

   _____

Multiple Choice

_____ 7. Which is the most typical tempo structure for a symphony?
        a. fast, moderate triple dance, slow, fast
        b. slow, fast, fast, moderate triple dance
        c. fast, slow, moderate triple dance, fast

_____ 8. The third movement of the nineteenth-century symphony is most
        likely in:
        a. scherzo form.
        b. sonata-allegro form.
        c. theme and variations form.

_____ 9. The concerto most typically has:
   a. one movement.
   b. three movements.
   c. four movements.

10. In what ways did nineteenth-century composers change the overall form of the symphony? _____

_____

11. How does the form of the first movement of a concerto differ from sonata-allegro form in a symphony? _____

_____

_____

12. Who were some of the major contributors to the Romantic concerto?

_____

13. How do you account for the rise in virtuosity in the nineteenth century?

_____

_____

14. Since absolute forms such as the symphony and the concerto generally have no program, what gives them their sense of shape and meaning?

_____

_____

_____

61. *Listen* Brahms and Dvořák as Symphonists

Brahms: Symphony No. 3 in F major, Third Movement (**LG** 50 Chr; 27 Sh;
11 Std; *e***LG**)
*Dvořák: Symphony No. 9 in E minor, First Movement (**LG** 51 Chr; 12 Std; *e***LG**)

Exercises

Listen to the third movement of Brahms's Symphony No. 3 while following
the Listening Guide, then answer questions 1–7.

1. How many symphonies did Brahms write? _____

   Why did he wait until late in his life to write symphonies?

   _____

   _____

2. What is the composer's musical motto heard in Symphony No. 3?

   _____

3. How many movements does this symphony have? _____

4. What is unusual about the third movement? _____

   _____

5. How would you describe the musical character of this third movement's:

   opening section? _____

   middle section? _____

6. What is changed in the restatement (return of opening theme)?

   _____

7. How is this symphony cyclical? _____

   _____

   Name another cyclical symphony.

   _____

*Listen to the first movement of Dvořák's Symphony No. 9 (*From the New World*), following the Listening Guide, then answer questions 8–15.

8. How did this symphony get its subtitle *From the New World*?

   _____

9. What is "American" about the work? _____

   _____

10. On what epic poem is it loosely based? _____

    _____ Who is the poet? _____

11. Is this symphony in standard sonata-cycle form? _____

    Are the keys of the movements standard? _____

12. How has Dvořák achieved a folklike character in themes of the first

    movement? _____

    _____

13. What works did Dvořák write that could be considered nationalistic?

    _____

    _____

14. Describe what mood or picture you envisage when you listen to this
    movement of the *New World* Symphony.

    _____

    _____

    _____

> ### 62. *Explore* Dvořák's Influence on African-American Art Music
> CP 12 Chr/Sh; 4 Std

Exercises

Complete the following questions.

1. What types of traditional music interested Dvořák during his years in America? _____

   _____

2. What famous American poem is loosely the basis for Dvořák's *New World* Symphony?_____

3. Which spiritual did Dvořák like especially?

   _____

4. What challenge did Dvořák issue to American composers?

   _____

   _____

   _____

5. For what is Dvořák's student Henry Burleigh known today?

   _____

   _____

   _____

6. Which well-known African-American composer rose to Dvořák's challenge? _____

   How did he accomplish this? _____

   _____

   _____

   _____

7. Which white American composer is famous for his wedding of jazz to art music? _____

   Which work demonstrates this?_____

Listening Assignment

Listen to a recording of one movement from William Grant Still's *Afro-American Symphony* and describe how it imitates blues, jazz, spirituals, or other traditional African-American music styles and instruments. (Or listen to Still's Suite for Violin and Piano, third movement; Gershwin's *Rhapsody in Blue* or Concerto in F; or an arrangement for a spiritual.) Consider what musical elements of African-American music influenced this work.

Or visit the Web site (www.wwnorton.com/enjoy), read the Cultural Perspective, and describe below the path you chose through the Web links.

Selection: _____

Composer: _____

_____

_____

_____

_____

_____

_____

_____

_____

_____

_____

_____

_____

_____

_____

_____

_____

_____

_____

_____

_____

_____

_____

---

63. *Listen* Felix Mendelssohn and the Romantic Concerto
*Felix Mendelssohn: Violin Concerto in E minor, First Movement (**LG** 52 Chr; 13 Std; *e***LG**)

Exercises

*Listen to the first movement of Felix Mendelssohn's Violin Concerto in E minor while following the Listening Guide, then answer the following questions.

   1. What is the tempo scheme for the movements of this concerto?

      _____

      Does this fit the Classical scheme? _____

   2. What is unusual about the form of the first movement? _____

      _____

   3. Is there an orchestral exposition?_____

   4. How would you describe the first theme?_____

      _____

   5. Where does the cadenza occur? _____

      Is this the normal place? _____

   6. Is there a break before the second movement? _____

   7. For whom was this concerto written? _____

   8. Was the cadenza improvised or written by the composer?

      _____

   9. What effect does the minor key have on the character of the first

      movement? _____

      _____

  10. What are some Classical elements of this work? _____

      _____

      _____

  11. What are some Romantic elements? _____

      _____

      _____

12. What was Mendelssohn's early family life like? _____

_____

How did his upbringing contribute to his love of music?

_____

13. Which earlier composers did Mendelssohn revere?

_____

14. Which major work by a Baroque composer did he revive?

_____

15. Besides composing, what other musical roles did Mendelssohn take on?

_____

16. Which famous conservatory did he found? _____

17. Mendelssohn died at a very young age, just months after the premature
    death of which beloved family member? _____

18. What other orchestral works did Mendelssohn write? _____

_____

19. His most famous incidental music, based on Shakespeare, was

_____

20. Name a well-known oratorio by Mendelssohn. _____

21. In which other genres did he compose? _____

_____

64. *Review* The Rise of Classical Composition in America
Chap. 58 Chr; 53 Sh; 29 Std

Exercises

Complete the following questions.

1. What musical tradition prevailed in America in the nineteenth century?

   _____

2. Which American composer from New Orleans set African-American
   and Creole styles into his music? _____

3. Name several prominent New England composers who also held
   important university professorships. Cite one work by each.

   Composer: _____   _____

   University: _____   _____

   Work: _____   _____

4. Which composer set Native-American tunes in his music?

   _____

5. Who was the most prominent woman composer of the New England
   School? _____ Name several of her works.

   _____

6. What composition inspired Beach's Symphony in E minor?

   _____

7. Why is her symphony significant?

   _____

8. What folk styles did she incorporate into this symphony?

   _____

*9. Which of her works reflect her interest in bird songs?

   _____

*10. Where did she write these piano works?

   _____

11. Why did she prefer to be known as Mrs. H. H. A. Beach?

   _____

*Listen to the second movement of Amy Beach's Violin Sonata in A minor (**LG** 53 Chr; 14 Std; *e***LG**) while following the Listening Guide, then answer questions 12–21.

12. When was this sonata written? _____

13. Where and by whom was it premiered?

_____

14. What was the reaction of the critics to the sonata?

_____

15. Does the sonata generally conform to the multimovement cycle?

_____

16. Is it normal for the second movement to be a scherzo? _____

17. Is it normal for a scherzo to be set in duple meter? _____

18. Describe the nature of the opening theme of the scherzo.

_____

19. Describe the mood of the trio. _____

_____

20. What is a perpetuum mobile? _____

Does this phrase apply to this movement? _____

21. What European composer's techniques seem to have influenced Beach

in this sonata? _____ What techniques?

_____

65. *Explore* Women and Music: A Feminist Perspective
CP 13 Chr/Sh; 5 Std

Exercises

Complete the following questions.

1. What was the typical nineteenth-century attitude toward women and their artistic creativity? _____

   _____

2. Name two female novelists and the pen names under which they wrote.

   _____

   _____

3. What were the concerns of the women's movement in the early twentieth century? _____

4. When did women gain the right to vote? _____

5. What contributions did composer Ethel Smyth make to the women's movement? _____

   _____

6. Which modern women composers have focused on the experiences of women? _____

7. What has been the general attitude toward women in popular music?

   _____

   _____

8. Which modern performers have tried to stop "female bashing" in popular music? _____

9. Do you think there is a "women's voice" expressed in music? _____ Why? _____

   _____

10. Do you think that biology, or gender, plays a role in the creative process? _____ Explain. _____

   _____

Listening Assignment

Select a recording of a modern female performer or of music by a modern female composer. Listen to the lyrics or read about the work and its inspiration. Comment below on whether there is a "women's voice" being expressed.

Or visit the Web site (www.wwnorton.com/enjoy), read the Cultural Perspective, and describe below the path you chose through the Web links.

_____

_____

_____

_____

_____

_____

_____

_____

_____

_____

_____

_____

_____

_____

_____

_____

_____

_____

_____

_____

_____

_____

_____

---

66. *Listen* Brahms and Romantic Choral Music
Brahms: *A German Requiem*, Fourth Movement (**LG** 50 Chr; 28 Sh; 15 Std; *e***LG**)

Exercises

Listen to the fourth movement of *A German Requiem* by Brahms while
following the Listening Guide, then answer questions 1–8.

1. What events in Brahms's life inspired him to write a requiem?

   _____

2. In what language is a Requiem Mass usually sung? _____

   With which church is it usually associated? _____

3. Rather than using the standard text of the Requiem Mass, Brahms
   constructed his own. What sources did he use?

   _____

   _____

   _____

   _____

4. What musical forces does it take to perform *A German Requiem*?

   _____

   _____

5. What is the text source for the fourth movement? _____

   From which part of the Bible is this text taken? _____

6. What is the mood established by this movement? _____

   How does Brahms suggest this character through music?

   _____

   _____

7. What unifies the fourth movement of this Requiem?

   _____

   _____

8. Brahms marks this movement "moderately agitated" (*mässig bewegt*).
   Does this indication seem appropriate for any part of the movement?

   _____

Complete the following questions.

9. What factors contributed to the rise of amateur choral groups in the nineteenth century? _____

_____

_____

_____

10. What are the main choral forms used in the nineteenth century?

_____

11. What are the standard voice parts in a choir? _____

_____

12. What is a part song? _____

_____

13. Which Romantic composers contributed significantly to the choral music literature? _____

_____

14. Is it true that singing in a chorus takes less skill than playing an instrument in an orchestra? _____

Do you have any choral singing experience? _____

If so, with which group(s)? _____

_____

---

67. *Review* Romantic Opera
Chap. 60 Chr; 55 Sh; 31 Std

Exercises

Complete the following questions.

1. Describe the following parts of an opera, giving consideration to musical style and purpose within the plot. You may wish to refer back to an earlier chapter (21 Chr/Sh).

   a. aria: _____

   _____

   b. recitative: _____

   _____

   c. chorus: _____

   _____

   d. ensemble: _____

   _____

2. What is the role of the orchestra in an opera? _____

   _____

3. What is a libretto, and who writes it? _____

   _____

Match the following styles of opera with their definitions.

_____ 4. grand opera   a. light German opera featuring spoken dialogue

_____ 5. opéra comique   b. Italian version of comic opera

_____ 6. Singspiel   c. hybrid opera type with appealing melodies
                                 and romantic, dramatic spectacle

_____ 7. opera seria   d. French opera style, featuring historical
                                 subjects and huge forces

_____ 8. opera buffa   e. Italian singing style featuring florid lines and
                                 pure voices

_____ 9. bel canto   f. French comic opera, with simple plots and
                                 spoken dialogue

_____ 10. lyric opera   g. Italian serious opera

Match the following well-known operas with their composers (look up the principal works of these composers in the text).

_____ 11. *Die Meistersinger von Nürnberg*   a. Giuseppe Verdi

_____ 12. *Aida*   b. Richard Wagner

_____ 13. *La traviata*

_____ 14. *Siegfried*

_____ 15. *Tristan and Isolde*

_____ 16. *The Flying Dutchman*

_____ 17. *Otello*

18. What makes an opera "exotic"? _____

    _____

    Name an example. _____

19. Name an opera composed by a woman. _____

    Who was the composer? _____

    What was the basis of the plot? _____

20. Which famous soprano was known as "the Swedish nightingale"?

    _____

    Who managed her career in America?_____

21. What was the relationship between Maria Malibran and Pauline Viardot?

    _____

22. Which composers' works did they specialize in singing?

    Malibran: _____

    Viardot: _____

23. Did opera further the careers of women musicians in the Romantic

    era? _____ Explain. _____

    _____

    _____

---

68. *Listen* Verdi and Wagner

Verdi: *Rigoletto,* Act III, excerpt (**LG** 55 Chr; 29 Sh; 16 Std; *e***LG**)
Wagner: *Die Walküre,* Act III, Finale (**LG** 56 Chr; 30 Sh; 17 Std; *e***LG**)

Exercises

Listen to the excerpt from Verdi's *Rigoletto* while following the Listening Guide, then answer questions 1–10.

1. What literary work provided the basis for *Rigoletto?*

   _____

2. When and where is the story of *Rigoletto* set? _____

   _____

3. Describe the melodic style of the aria "La donna è mobile."

   _____

4. What is the Duke's attitude toward women? _____

   _____

5. Describe the emotions each character is expressing in the quartet.

   The Duke: _____

   Maddalena: _____

   Gilda: _____

   Rigoletto: _____

6. Why do you think Verdi's operas have remained so popular?

   _____

ABOUT THE COMPOSER

7. In what country was Verdi born? _____

8. Which Verdi operas were inspired by Shakespeare?

   _____

9. Which of his operas could be described as "exotic"?

   _____

10. What was his last great opera? _____

Listen to the excerpt from Wagner's *Die Walküre* while following the Listening Guide, then answer questions 11–23.

11. What is the basis for the story of this opera? _____

12. Who is Wotan? _____

    Brünnhilde? _____

13. Describe the following musical themes in your own words.

    *Wotan's farewell: _____

    Wotan's invocation of Loge: _____

    "Magic fire" music: _____

    "Magic sleep" music: _____

True or False

____ 14. Wagner's operas reflect his desire to link music and drama closely.

____ 15. His operas have the same individual components—arias, recitatives, and ensembles—as Verdi's.

____ 16. *The Ring of the Nibelung* is a cycle of four operas.

____ 17. Wagner strove to achieve an endless melody that was melded to the German language.

____ 18. The orchestra was unimportant to Wagner's music dramas.

____ 19. Wagner employed recurring themes called leitmotifs.

____ 20. Wagner's harmonic style was a conservative, diatonic one.

21. What are some of Wagner's operas written prior to *The Ring*?

    _____

    _____

22. What music festival was established for the performance of Wagner's

    operas? _____

23. With whom did Wagner find happiness late in his life?

    _____

---

69. *Explore* The Lure of Spain
CP 14 Chr/Sh; 6 Std

Exercises

Complete the following questions.

1. What culture is featured in Bizet's opera *Carmen*? _____

   In which country is the opera set? _____

2. What elements of *Carmen* did nineteenth-century audiences find

   shocking? _____

3. What could be viewed as "exotic" about Bizet's *Carmen*?

   _____

   _____

   _____

4. Explain the focus of the nineteenth-century movement known as

   naturalism. _____

   _____

   Which French writer was a leader in this movement? _____

5. What are the musical characteristics of flamenco music?

   _____

   _____

   _____

   What instruments are used in flamenco performance? _____

   _____

   What musical culture influenced flamenco singing style?

   _____

6. What is a habañera? _____

   What is its origin? _____

7. Which twentieth-century Latin American dance form did the habañera

   influence? _____ What is the character of this dance?

   _____

Essay

Locate a recorded example or video of flamenco music, listen to a selection, and describe as many elements of its style as you can—especially its rhythm, melody, and instruments. If you have a video, describe the dance movements as well as the music.

Or visit the Web site (www.wwnorton.com/enjoy), read the Cultural Perspective, and describe below the path you chose through the Web links.

_____

_____

_____

_____

_____

_____

_____

_____

_____

_____

_____

_____

_____

_____

_____

_____

_____

_____

_____

_____

_____

_____

_____

_____

_____

---

70. *Listen* Late Romantic Opera and Exoticism
*Bizet: *Carmen*, Act I, excerpt (**LG** 57 Chr; 18 Std; *e***LG**)
  Puccini: *Madame Butterfly*, "Un bel di" (**LG** 58 Chr; 31 Sh; 19 Std; *e***LG**)
  Japanese Kouta: *A White Fan* (**LG** 59 Chr; 32 Sh; 20 Std; *e***LG**)

Exercises

*Listen to the excerpt from Bizet's *Carmen* while following the Listening Guide, then answer questions 1–8.

1. What is the literary basis for *Carmen?* _____

_____

2. How does Bizet evoke the feeling of a march in Act I?

_____

3. What role does the chorus play in Act I of *Carmen?*

_____

_____

4. What kind of rhythmic accompaniment is heard in Carmen's aria?

_____

5. What is seductive about this character and her music?

_____

_____

6. Is Carmen a likable character? _____ Explain. _____

_____

7. What gives this opera its dramatic impact? _____

_____

8. In your opinion, what accounts for the popularity of this opera?

_____

_____

Listen to "Un bel di" from Puccini's opera *Madame Butterfly* while following the Listening Guide, then answer questions 9–15.

9. What is the basis for Puccini's opera *Madame Butterfly?*

_____

_____

139

10. At what point in the story does Butterfly sing the aria "Un bel di"?

_____

11. What gives this aria its highly dramatic mood? _____

_____

12. How does the opera *Madame Butterfly* end? _____

_____

13. What is exotic about *Madame Butterfly*? _____

_____

14. What other composers carried on the late-Romantic Italian operatic

tradition? _____

15. What was the movement known as *verismo*? _____

_____

Listen to the Japanese kouta *A White Fan* (*Hakusen no*) while following the Listening Guide, then answer questions 16–21.

16. What is a geisha? _____

_____

What would be the closest Western equivalent? _____

17. What kind of musical training was essential for a Japanese geisha?

_____

_____

18. What is a kouta? _____

19. For what occasion(s) would the kouta *A White Fan* be sung? _____

_____

20. Describe the vocal line of *A White Fan*. _____

_____

21. What instrument accompanies the voice in this song?

_____

How is it played? _____

71. *Review* Tchaikovsky and the Ballet
Chap. 65 Chr; 59 Sh; 36 Std

Exercises

True or False

_____ 1. Renaissance entertainments included elaborate dance sequences as part of theatrical productions.

_____ 2. Classical ballet was first developed in the Romantic era by the Russians.

_____ 3. Stravinsky and Diaghilev were famous Russian dancers.

_____ 4. The *pas de deux*, or dance for two, developed in Russia by the choreographer Petipa, is a standard element of classical ballet.

_____ 5. Tchaikovsky and Petipa worked together on *The Nutcracker*.

Complete the following questions.

6. What three well-known ballets did Tchaikovsky write?

a. _____

b. _____

c. _____

7. *The Nutcracker* was based on a story originally written by the Romantic

writer _____ and expanded by

_____.

ABOUT THE COMPOSER

8. What teaching position did Tchaikovsky hold in Russia?

_____

9. How did Tchaikovsky feel about his homosexuality?

_____

10. What role did Nadezhda von Meck play in the composer's life?

_____

11. What was the reaction of Western audiences to Tchaikovsky's music?

_____

_____

141

12. In addition to ballet, in which other musical genres did Tchaikovsky write? _____

_____

13. What is the setting for *The Nutcracker?* _____

_____

14. Who are the main characters? _____

_____

15. How do the "exotic" Arab and Chinese dances fit into the story of the ballet? _____

_____

16. How does Tchaikovsky set a different mood for each dance?

_____

17. Describe the character of each of the following dances.

March: _____

*Dance of the Sugar Plum Fairy: _____

_____

*Trepak: _____

18. Have you ever seen a performance of *The Nutcracker?* _____

If yes, was it ___ live, ___ on TV, or ___ on video?

Did you enjoy it? _____ What do you think accounts for the continued popularity of this classical ballet?

_____

_____

_____

---

72. *Review* The Post-Romantic Era and Impressionism
Trans. IV Chr/Sh/Std; **Chap.** 66 Chr/Std; 60 Sh

Exercises

Complete the following questions.

1. Give the approximate dates of the post-Romantic era. _____

2. Which Italian operatic composers can be associated with post-

   Romanticism? _____

3. Which Germanic composers can be associated with post-Romanticism?

   _____

4. List some post-Romantic characteristics heard in the music of these

   composers. _____

   _____

5. What are some of the national schools that rose to prominence in this

   era? _____

Multiple Choice

____ 6. Which is NOT true of the origins of Impressionism?
     a. It was first a term denoting scorn of the new style.
     b. The coining of the term was based on a painting by Claude Monet.
     c. The style was first popular in Italy.
     d. A school of artists developed, all wishing to capture first
        impressions on canvas.

____ 7. Who among these is NOT an Impressionist painter?
     a. Paul Klee   c. Edgar Degas
     b. Camille Pissarro   d. Auguste Renoir

____ 8. In poetry, the parallel movement toward suggestion rather than
        direct description was:
     a. Expressionism.   c. Symbolism.
     b. New Romanticism.   d. minimalism.

____ 9. Which American poet strongly influenced the literary movement
        referred to in the previous question?
     a. Charles Baudelaire   c. Stéphane Mallarmé
     b. Edgar Allan Poe   d. Paul Verlaine

10. What were some goals of Impressionist painters? _____

   _____

   _____

143

11. Describe the characteristics of Impressionist painting in your own words, based on the Monet painting *Impression: Sun Rising*, reproduced in your text. _____

_____

_____

12. Characterize the musical elements of Impressionist music below.

Melody/scales: _____

_____

Rhythm/meter: _____

_____

Harmony/dissonance: _____

_____

Form: _____

_____

13. In what ways did non-Western music influence Impressionism?

_____

_____

14. In what ways did Impressionism look back to earlier musical styles?

_____

_____

15. Which composer best exemplifies musical Impressionism?

_____

73. *Listen* Mahler, Debussy, and Ravel

*Mahler: *The Song of the Earth*, Third Movement (**LG** 61 Chr/Std; *e*LG)
  Debussy: *Prelude to "The Afternoon of a Faun"* (**LG** 62 Chr/Std; 34 Sh; *e*LG)
  *Ravel: *Feria*, from A *Spanish Rhapsody* (**LG** 63 Chr/Std; *e*LG)

Exercises

*Listen to the third movement from Mahler's *The Song of the Earth* while
following the Listening Guide, then answer questions 1–4.

1. What is the literary basis for *The Song of the Earth*?

   _____

2. What is the medium (performing forces) for this song cycle?

   _____

3. How does Mahler evoke the sounds of Chinese music in this work?

   _____

   _____

4. How does the text evoke images of China? _____

   _____

Listen to Debussy's *Prelude to "The Afternoon of a Faun"* while following the
Listening Guide, then answer questions 5–9.

5. What is the literary source for this Debussy work?

   _____

6. Briefly summarize the program for this work. _____

   _____

   _____

7. In your opinion, how does Debussy musically evoke images from the

   poem? _____

   _____

   _____

8. What Impressionistic traits do you hear in this work?

   Melody/rhythm: _____

   Harmony/texture: _____

   Form: _____

Timbre/color: _____

Other: _____

9. How does Debussy slightly vary the return of the opening material?

_____

_____

*Listen to the *Feria* from Ravel's *Spanish Rhapsody* while following the Listening Guide, then answer questions 10–18.

10. Which best describes the overall form of Ravel's *Spanish Rhapsody?*

_____ symphony _____ program symphony _____ suite

11. What is Spanish about the work? _____

12. The third movement is a habañera. Where have we studied this dance form? _____

13. What dance form is heard in the *Feria?* _____

Describe its character. _____

14. How did Ravel know these Spanish dance types? _____

_____

15. What are some of the instrumental effects that make this movement sound "exotic"? _____

_____

16. What is the overall form of the movement? _____

17. How does Ravel's musical style differ from that of Debussy?

_____

_____

_____

18. List some other works by Ravel that were inspired by the musics of other cultures. _____

_____

_____

74. *Explore* The Paris World Exhibition of 1889: A Cultural Awakening

CP 15 Chr/Sh/Std

Exercises

Complete the following questions.

1. What famous monument was built for the Paris World Exhibition of 1889? _____

2. What is a gamelan orchestra? _____

   _____

   _____

   From where did the gamelan that Debussy heard come? _____

3. What elements of gamelan music did Debussy try to imitate in his composition? _____

   _____

   _____

4. Which other countries were represented by musicians at this world exhibition? _____

   _____

   _____

5. What Middle Eastern styles of dancing were seen at this event?

   _____

6. What is a cakewalk? _____

   _____

   Where did it originate? _____

7. What other traditional music styles influenced Debussy?

   _____

   _____

8. What world music styles influenced the composer Maurice Ravel?

   _____

   _____

Listening Assignment

Locate a recording or video of a gamelan (from Java or Bali) in your library, or ask your instructor for one from the Music Example Bank. Listen to a selection and describe the music below. Be sure to read any notes available about the work.

Which country is the gamelan from? _____

What are the instruments heard? Describe how they sound and comment on the musical style (melody, rhythm, harmony, texture).

Or visit the Web site (www.wwnorton.com/enjoy), read the Cultural Perspective, and describe below the path you chose through the Web links.

_____

_____

_____

_____

_____

_____

_____

_____

_____

_____

_____

_____

_____

_____

_____

_____

_____

_____

_____

_____

_____

_____

_____

_____

> ### 75. *Review* Elements of Twentieth-Century Musical Style
> **Chaps.** 68–69 Chr/Std; 61–62 Sh

Exercises

Multiple Choice

_____ 1. In which element of music was primitivism most evident?
   a. melody
   b. rhythm
   c. texture
   d. harmony

_____ 2. Which statement is NOT true of Expressionism?
   a. It was principally a French movement.
   b. It attempted to probe the subconscious.
   c. It defied traditional notions of beauty.
   d. It portrayed images in distortion.

_____ 3. Which is most typical of Expressionist music?
   a. conjunct, symmetrical melodies
   b. instruments used in extreme high and low registers
   c. consonant, tonal harmonies
   d. regular meters and rhythms

_____ 4. Which is most typical of the New Classicism?
   a. an emotional, expressive style
   b. a focus on program music
   c. a preference for absolute music
   d. an attempt to bring music and poetry closer

Match the following early-twentieth-century figures with the correct description.

_____ 5. Paul Gauguin   a. Expressionist composer

_____ 6. Pablo Picasso   b. Expressionist writer

_____ 7. Franz Kafka   c. Expressionist painter

_____ 8. Joan Miró   d. French painter drawn to primitive
                                       subjects

_____ 9. Arnold Schoenberg   e. Surrealist painter

_____ 10. Oskar Kokoschka   f. Cubist painter

11. Which early-twentieth-century figures were influential to avant-garde

   composer John Cage? _____

Match the following musical terms with their definitions.

_____ 12. polyrhythm

a. a particular arrangement of the twelve chromatic tones

_____ 13. dissonant counterpoint

b. the use of two or more keys together

_____ 14. polytonality

c. music based on the twelve-tone method

_____ 15. serial music

d. the simultaneous use of several rhythmic patterns

_____ 16. tone row

e. the use of dissonant intervals to set musical lines apart

_____ 17. atonality

f. the rejection of any key or tonality

True or False

_____ 18. In twentieth-century music, dissonances do not always resolve.

_____ 19. Orchestras grew even larger in the early twentieth century.

_____ 20. Twentieth-century melodies are generally more difficult to sing than those of the Romantic era.

_____ 21. The use of triads continued to predominate early-twentieth-century music.

_____ 22. Schoenberg is generally credited with founding the twelve-tone method of composition.

_____ 23. Tone rows were often transposed to other pitch levels.

_____ 24. Early-twentieth-century music remained consonant to the ear.

_____ 25. Duple, triple, and quadruple meter were the norm in the early twentieth century.

_____ 26. Inversion refers to the mirror-image movement of a line, wherein each interval moves in the opposite direction from the original.

_____ 27. Dark or low instruments were explored by early-twentieth-century composers.

---

76. *Listen* The Music of Stravinsky

Stravinsky: *The Rite of Spring*, Part II, excerpts (**LG** 64 Chr/Std; 35 Sh; *e***LG**)
* Stravinsky: *The Royal March*, from The *Soldier's Tale* (**LG** 65 Chr/Std)

Exercises

Listen to the excerpts from Stravinsky's *The Rite of Spring* while following the Listening Guide, then answer questions 1–6.

1. Name the three ballets Stravinsky composed for Diaghilev and the

   Ballet Russe. _____

   _____

2. Name three musical characteristics of *The Rite of Spring* that shaped a

   new musical language for the twentieth century. _____

   _____

   _____

3. What makes *The Rite of Spring* a nationalistic work?

   _____

   _____

   _____

4. Describe how Stravinsky expanded the orchestra in *The Rite of Spring*.

   _____

   _____

5. Describe the story of the ballet, in particular the action in Part II.

   _____

   _____

   _____

   _____

6. How does Stravinsky evoke primitivism in *The Rite of Spring*?

   _____

   _____

   _____

*Listen to *The Royal March* from Stravinsky's *The Soldier's Tale* and answer the following questions.

7. What is the literary basis for *The Soldier's Tale?* _____

_____

8. What is neoclassical about this work? _____

_____

9. Describe the rhythmic nature of *The Royal March* from *The Soldier's Tale.*

_____

_____

10. What is the form of *The Royal March?* _____

ABOUT THE COMPOSER

11. Where was Stravinsky born? _____

12. Where was *The Rite of Spring* primiered? _____

13. Where did Stravinsky live after World War I? _____

After World War II? _____

14. Late in life, Stravinsky wrote twelve-tone compositions. Name one using

this compositional procedure: _____

15. Name a choral work by Stravinsky: _____

An opera: _____

---

77. *Listen* Schoenberg, Berg, and Webern

Schoenberg: *Pierrot lunaire*, Nos. 18 and *21 (**LG** 66 Chr/Std; 36 Sh; *e*LG)
*Berg: *Wozzeck,* Act III, Scene 4, Interlude, and Scene 5 (**LG** 67 Chr/Std; *e*LG)
*Webern: Symphony, Opus 21, Second Movement (**LG** 68 Chr/Std; *e*LG)

Exercises

Listen to the selections from Schoenberg's *Pierrot lunaire* while following the Listening Guide, then answer questions 1–9.

1. What new singing style did Schoenberg employ in *Pierrot lunaire?*

   _____ Explain this style. _____

   _____

   What were Schoenberg's goals in using this style? _____

   _____

2. What is the literary source of the poems in *Pierrot lunaire?*

   _____

3. What is the medium for this work? _____

   _____

4. With what is the main character preoccupied in these poems?

   _____

5. What is Expressionistic about this work? _____

   _____

6. Describe the harmony and texture of *Der Mondfleck* (No. 18).

   _____

*7. How are these elements treated in *O alter Duft* (No. 21)?

   _____

8. Schoenberg abandoned the traditional ordering of a work around a key

   center, resulting first in a style known as _____.

   He eventually devised a system using all twelve tones of the chromatic

   scale, known as _____. In which period does *Pierrot*

   lunaire fall? _____

9. What was the relationship of Schoenberg to composers Alban Berg and

   Anton Webern? _____

*Listen to the excerpt from Berg's opera *Wozzeck*, while following the Listening Guide, then answer questions 10–14.

10. What is the literary basis for the opera *Wozzeck?*

_____

11. What is Expressionistic about its subject and music?

_____

_____

12. How does the vocal line portray Wozzeck's state of mind?

_____

13. What is the emotional effect of the opera's closing scene?

_____

14. What was Berg's other opera? _____

*Listen to the second movement from Webern's Symphony, Op. 21, while following the Listening Guide, then answer questions 15–20.

15. What size orchestra does this work employ? _____

16. What is the musical technique *Klangfarbenmelodie?* _____

_____

How does this technique compare with pointillism in painting?

_____

17. What types of contrapuntal procedures occur in this movement?

_____

_____

18. Is this work _____ tonal, _____ atonal, or _____ serial?

19. What formal structures are employed in the work? _____

_____

20. How did Webern die? _____

_____

78. *Review* Nationalism in the Twentieth Century
Chaps. 74–75 Chr/Std; 65–66 Sh

Exercises

Match the following composers with their nationalistic school on the right.
You may use answers as many times as necessary.

_____ 1. Benjamin Britten   a. French school

_____ 2. Paul Hindemith   b. German school

_____ 3. Charles Ives   c. Russian school

_____ 4. Sergei Rachmaninoff   d. English school

_____ 5. Béla Bartók   e. Hungarian school

_____ 6. Carl Orff   f. Scandinavian school

_____ 7. Dmitri Shostakovich   g. American school

_____ 8. Francis Poulenc   h. Spanish school

_____ 9. Jean Sibelius

_____ 10. Sergei Prokofiev

_____ 11. Manuel de Falla

12. For each of the countries below, suggest a historical event or nationalistic
    theme or setting that either served or could have served as the basis
    for a musical composition.

    a. Russia: _____

    b. France: _____

    c. Germany: _____

    d. England: _____

    e. United States: _____

13. What were the goals of the French group known as "Les Six"?

    _____

    Who was the only female member of this group?_____

14. Name a composer and work linked to Jewish cultural origins.

    _____

    _____

True or False

_____ 15. The spiritual is of European origin.

_____ 16. The music of some European nationalist composers features folk elements.

_____ 17. Shape-note notation was designed for people who could not read music.

_____ 18. The American composer Charles Ives was from California.

19. Stephen Foster is known for his ballads, minstrel show tunes, and plantation songs. Name three of his works. _____

_____

20. Out of what tradition did American bands grow?

_____

21. What was the makeup of the original U.S. Marine Band?

_____

22. Who was America's most famous bandmaster? _____

Name two marches he composed. _____

_____

23. Which famous musical instrument inventor revolutionized the keys on brass instruments? _____

What well-known instrument did he invent? _____

24. Which New England composer was inspired by the hymns and patriotic songs he learned as a youth? _____

---

79. *Explore* Bartók—A Folk-Song Collector
CP 16 Chr/Sh/Std

Exercises

Complete the following questions.

1. What were the goals of composers Béla Bartók and Zoltán Kodály in collecting Eastern European folk songs? _____

_____

_____

2. What is an ethnomusicologist? _____

_____

3. What does it mean to do "fieldwork" in music? _____

_____

4. How was Bartók's art music influenced by the traditional music he collected? _____

_____

_____

5. What is an additive meter? _____

_____

_____

6. Describe the background of the Roma people and their musical traditions. _____

_____

_____

_____

What are Roma popularly called? _____

7. What nineteenth-century Hungarian composer was interested in Roma music? _____ What evidence do we have of this interest? _____

_____

Listening Assignment

Listen to a recording of modern Roma (Gypsy) music (find one in your library or ask your instructor for one from the Music Example Bank). Name the ensemble selected, list the instruments heard, and describe the musical style (melodic, rhythmic, harmonic, singing style).

Or visit the Web site (www.wwnorton.com/enjoy), read the Cultural Perspective, then describe below the path you chose through the Web links.

_____

_____

_____

_____

_____

_____

_____

_____

_____

_____

_____

_____

_____

_____

_____

_____

_____

_____

_____

_____

_____

_____

_____

_____

_____

_____

80. *Listen* Bartók and Ives
Bartók: *Concerto for Orchestra*, Fourth Movement (**LG** 69 Chr/Std; 37 Sh; *e***LG**)
*Ives: *The Things Our Fathers Loved* (**LG** 70 Chr/Std; *e***LG**)

Exercises

Listen to *Interrupted Intermezzo* from Bartók's *Concerto for Orchestra* while following the Listening Guide, then answer questions 1–12.

1. How can this orchestral work be a concerto even though it has no solo

   instrument? _____

   _____

2. When was it written? _____ Who commissioned it?

   _____

3. How many movements does the *Concerto for Orchestra* have? _____

4. What elements of folk music are captured in this work?

   _____

5. From which composer and work does Bartók borrow a theme in the

   fourth movement? _____

6. What is the general form of the fourth movement? _____

7. How would you describe the meter of the opening? _____

   _____

8. Is Bartók's music dissonant? _____ What is the effect?

   _____

ABOUT THE COMPOSER

9. What nationality was Bartók? _____

10. What attracted him to the folk music of his native land?

    _____

    _____

11. Name several of Bartók's most famous compositions.

    _____

    _____

12. Why did Bartók leave his homeland and come to America?

    _____

*Listen to *The Things Our Fathers Loved* by Ives while following the Listening Guide, then answer questions 13–18.

13. What tunes does Ives incorporate into this song?

_____

_____

    Which of the tunes do you recognize? _____

_____

14. How is Ives's music nationalistic? _____

_____

_____

15. How would you characterize his treatment of harmony?

_____

16. What familiar American images does this song bring to mind?

_____

_____

17. What are some of Ives's other nationalistic compositions?

_____

_____

18. Charles Ives is viewed today as one of the great twentieth-century American composers. How was his music received by the public during his lifetime?

_____

_____

---

81. *Explore* Music and the Patriotic Spirit
CP 17 Chr/Sh/Std

Exercises

Complete the following questions.

1. What famous tunes were sung during the Revolutionary and Civil Wars?

   _____

   _____

2. What Civil War song text was written by Julia Ward Howe?

   _____

3. Which twentieth-century songwriter provided the music and words to
   Over There? _____ During which war was this
   song popular? _____

4. Which well-known patriotic song, made famous by singer Kate Smith, is
   regarded as a second national anthem in the United States?

   _____

5. How have the tragic events of September 11, 2001 influenced the
   popularity of this song? _____

   _____

6. Describe when and by whom the lyrics for *The Star-Spangled Banner* were
   written. _____

   _____

   _____

7. Which national anthems can be viewed as songs of war or independence?

   _____

   _____

8. What is the origin of the tune to Austria's *Emperor's Hymn?*

   _____

   Which other country has adopted this song? _____

8. What is the Canadian national anthem? _____

   Who wrote it, and when? _____

161

Activity

Watch a video borrowed from the library or a video store of the 1942 film classic *Yankee Doodle Dandy*, starring James Cagney as George M. Cohan. Note which songs from the show had inspirational or patriotic texts. Describe the setting of the film and its patriotic focus.

Or visit the Web site (www.wwnorton.com/enjoy), read the Cultural Perspective, then describe below the path you chose through the Web links.

---

82. *Explore* Copland Looks West and South of the Border
CP 18 Chr/Sh/Std   🖳

Exercises

Complete the following questions.

1. What American themes did composer Aaron Copland incorporate in

   his music? _____

   _____

2. What aspects of cowboy life do their songs describe? _____

   _____

   _____

3. Name several historical American cowboys and cowgirls.

   _____

   _____

4. Who was the subject of the Broadway musical *Annie Get Your Gun?*

   _____

5. Who was the "yellow rose of Texas," and why was she famous?

   _____

   _____

   _____

   _____

6. Which American artist is well known for his cowboy bronzes?

   _____

7. Describe the Mexican jarabe. _____

   _____

   _____

8. Describe a mariachi ensemble. _____

   _____

   _____

Listening Assignment

Locate a recording of a Mexican mariachi ensemble. Listen to several selections and describe below the instruments heard, the melodic and rhythmic style, and any vocals heard.

Or visit the Web site (www.wwnorton.com/enjoy), read the Cultural Perspective, then describe below the path you chose through the Web links.

_____

_____

_____

_____

_____

_____

_____

_____

_____

_____

_____

_____

_____

_____

_____

_____

_____

_____

_____

_____

_____

_____

_____

_____

---

83. *Listen* Copland and Revueltas

Copland: *Street in a Frontier Town*, from *Billy the Kid* (**LG** 71 Chr/Std; 38 Sh; *e***LG**)
Revueltas: *Homenaje a Federico García Lorca*, Third Movement, *Son* (**LG** 72 Chr/Std; 39 Sh; *e***LG**)

Exercises

Listen to *Street in a Frontier Town* from Copland's *Billy the Kid* while following the Listening Guide, then answer questions 1–7.

1. Briefly describe the story of *Billy the Kid.* _____

   _____

   _____

2. Suggest how each musical element below supports the story.

   Melody: _____

   Rhythm/meter: _____

   Harmony: _____

   Choice of instruments: _____

   _____

3. How does the composer evoke a Mexican dance?

   _____

   _____

4. Do you recognize any of the tunes Copland uses in this work? _____

   If yes, which? _____

5. Does he use the tunes literally? _____ Explain. _____

   _____

6. List two other ballets by Copland and tell how each is nationalistic.

   a. _____

   _____

   b. _____

   _____

7. How did Copland gain his familiarity with American folk music?

   _____

   _____

   _____

165

Listen to Revueltas's *Homenaje a Federico García Lorca*, third movement, while following the Listening Guide, then answer questions 8–17.

8. What Mexican folk ensemble is alluded to in *Homenaje a Federico García Lorca?* _____

   How does Revueltas evoke this sound? _____

9. Who is Federico García Lorca and why did Revueltas wish to honor him?

   _____

   _____

10. 1. What is unusual about the makeup of the orchestra for this work?

    _____

11. What is the meaning of the title of the third movement (*Son*)?

    _____

12. How would you characterize the treatment of rhythm and meter in this work? _____

    _____

13. What term best describes the overall form of this movement?

    _____

ABOUT THE COMPOSER AND HIS TIME

14. What is "mestizo realism"?_____

    _____

15. Who were some other influential Mexican composers of this era?

    _____

16. How was Revueltas's music viewed in his day? _____

    _____

17. What is Revueltas's best known orchestral work? _____

    What was the inspiration for this work? _____

    _____

---

84. *Review* Early Jazz Styles
Chap. 76 Chr/Std; 67 Sh

Exercises

Complete the following questions.

1. What styles merged to form early jazz? _____

_____

2. What is ragtime? _____

_____

Who is considered the "king of ragtime"? _____

What famous rags did he write? _____

3. What were Joplin's musical goals for ragtime? _____

_____

4. In which classical genre did he compose? _____

What is his most famous work in this genre? _____

_____

_____

5. What is the typical poetic form of a blues text?

_____

_____

6. Write one verse of your own that could be sung to the blues.

_____

_____

_____

7. What is the standard musical form in blues? _____

_____

8. What is a "blue note"? _____

9. Name a great female blues singer. _____

10. Which instruments would generally be heard in New Orleans jazz?

_____

_____

11. What is scat singing? _____

    _____

    Who is credited with inventing it? _____

True or False

_____ 12. New Orleans-style jazz spread across the country in the 1920s.

_____ 13. Lillian Hardin was a jazz pianist and composer.

_____ 14. Louis Armstrong was a noted jazz trombone player.

_____ 15. Ella Fitzgerald was a virtuoso scat singer.

_____ 16. Billie Holiday sang only with Black performers.

_____ 17. A vocable is a text syllable with no meaning.

  18. What was so shocking about Billie Holiday's famous song *Strange Fruit*?

    _____

    _____

    _____

85. *Explore* The Roots of Jazz
CP 19 Chr/Sh/Std

Exercises

Complete the following questions.

1. From which cultures does jazz draw musical elements?

   _____

   _____

2. What singing styles still heard in certain African-American communities have African origins? _____

   _____

3. What is a work song? _____

   _____

4. What is a spiritual? _____

   _____

5. In which American city was jazz "born"? _____

6. What characterized nineteenth-century African-American music?

   _____

   _____

   _____

7. How did rural, or country, blues develop? _____

   _____

   _____

8. Describe ragtime and its rise to popularity. _____

   _____

   _____

   _____

9. Which art music composers were highly influenced by ragtime?

   _____

   _____

169

Listening Assignment

Listen to a recording of a white or African-American spiritual, a vocal blues by Bessie Smith or Billie Holiday, or a rag by Scott Joplin. List the work selected and its style, and describe its melodic and harmonic styles, its rhythm and meter, its form, its text (if any), and its instrumentation.

Or visit the Web site (www.wwnorton.com/enjoy), read the Cultural Perspective, and describe below the path you chose through the Web links.

_____

_____

_____

_____

_____

_____

_____

_____

_____

_____

_____

_____

_____

_____

_____

_____

_____

_____

_____

_____

_____

_____

_____

_____

---

86. *Listen* Ragtime, Blues, and Early Jazz
Joplin: *Maple Leaf Rag* (**LG** 73 Chr/Std; 40 Sh; *e***LG**)
Holiday: *Billie's Blues* (**LG** 74 Chr/Std; 41 Sh)

Exercises

Listen to the recording of Scott Joplin playing his own *Maple Leaf Rag* on your CD set while following the Listening Guide, then answer questions 1–6.

    1. What stylistic element gives ragtime its name? _____

    _____

    2. What is a strain? _____

       How long is each strain in *Maple Leaf Rag*? _____

    3. Outline the form of the work. _____

       Can you hear the repeated sections? _____

    4. How did Joplin record this work? _____

    _____

    5. Which strain is heard in a new key (other than the tonic)? _____

    6. What is the role of the left hand (bass part) in this piece? _____

    _____

       The right hand? _____

    _____

Listen to *Billie's Blues* by Billie Holiday while following the Listening Guide, then answer questions 7–12.

    7. What is the form of *Billie's Blues*? _____

    8. Which chorus is a typical blues verse in text structure? _____

    9. Which solo instruments can be heard in the fourth and fifth choruses

       of *Billie's Blues*? _____

    _____

   10. What kind of pitch inflections are typical in the blues? _____

    _____

11. How do each of the soloists (Holiday, Shaw, and Berrigan) contribute
    their own styles to this performance of *Billie's Blues?*

    Holiday: _____

    Shaw: _____

    Berrigan: _____

12. What jazz performers influenced Holiday as she developed her own
    style? _____

87. *Review* The Swing Era and Later Jazz Styles
Chap. 77 Chr/Std; 68 Sh

Exercises

Complete the following questions.

1. What decades are associated with the swing, or big band, era?

   _____

2. What was the economic situation in the United States during this era?

   _____

3. What jazz pianist/composer played a major role in the development of

   the swing era? _____

4. Name some musicians/composers associated with each style listed below:

   bebop: _____

   cool jazz: _____

   West coast jazz: _____

5. What term refers to the merger of classical art music and jazz? _____

   Who is credited with this concept? _____

6. What is fusion? _____

   Name some fusion artists. _____

   _____

7. Name two American composers who have successfully merged classical

   and jazz styles in their compositions. _____

   _____

8. Describe Gershwin's songs. _____

   _____

9. How do his songs differ from his instrumental works? _____

10. Describe the diversity of classical and jazz elements found in Baker's

    compositions. _____

    _____

    _____

11. What theme is prevalent in Baker's music? _____

12. Name some musical genres that stem from the African-American
    experience. _____

    _____

    _____

88. *Listen* Big Band and Bebop
*Strayhorn/Ellington: *Take the A Train* (**LG** 75 Chr/Std; *e***LG**)
 Gillespie/Parker: *A Night in Tunisia* (**LG** 76 Chr/Std; 42 Sh; *e***LG**)

Exercises

*Listen to *Take the A Train* by Strayhorn/Ellington while following the Listening Guide, then answer questions 1–6.

1. What is the form of *Take the A Train?* _____

2. What is the medium? _____

3. What solo instruments are featured in *Take the A Train?*

   _____

   Who are the soloists on this recording? _____

   _____

4. How is "call and response" used in this piece? _____

   _____

5. What effects can be heard in the trumpet solo? _____

   _____

6. What makes assigning the authorship of this piece to Strayhorn or

   Ellington difficult? _____

   _____

Listen to *A Night in Tunisia* by Gillespie/Parker while following the Listening Guide, then answer questions 7–13.

7. Which two jazz legends are featured in our recording of *A Night in*

   Tunisia? _____

   What instruments do they play? _____

8. Who composed the tune? _____

   What does he play? _____

9. What size ensemble plays this jazz selection? _____

10. In bebop and other jazz styles, the tune is presented first, followed by:

   _____

11. What is a break, and where does one occur in *A Night in Tunisia?*

_____

_____

12. What is a jazz riff? _____

_____

13. How would you describe Parker's style of improvisation? _____

_____

> ### 89. *Listen* Gershwin, Baker, and the Merger of Classical and Popular Styles
> Gershwin: Piano Prelude No. 1 (**LG** 77 Chr/Std; 43 Sh; *e***LG**)
> Baker: *Sometimes I Feel Like a Motherless Child*, from *Through This Vale of Tears*
> (**LG** 78 Chr/Std; 44 Sh; *e***LG**)

Exercises

Listen to Gershwin's Piano Prelude No. 1 while following the Listening Guide, then answer questions 1–5.

1. What is the form of Gershwin's Piano Prelude No. 1? _____

2. What does "Allegro ben ritmato e deciso" mean? _____

   _____

3. Who transcribed this piece for violin and piano? _____

   What is the original instrumentation of this work? _____

4. What jazz elements can be heard in Piano Prelude No. 1? _____

   _____

5. What other instrumental works by Gershwin combine elements of jazz

   with classical forms? _____

   _____

Listen to Baker's *Sometimes I Feel Like a Motherless Child* from *Through This Vale of Tears* while following the Listening Guide, then answer questions 6–11.

6. What genre best describes Baker's *Through This Vale of Tears*?

   _____

7. Who inspired him to write this composition? _____

8. *Through This Vale of Tears* is scored for: _____

   _____

9. From which writers/sources did Baker draw texts for the songs in

   Through This Vale of Tears? _____

   _____

10. What is the basis for Baker's setting of *Sometimes I Feel Like a Motherless*

    Child? _____

    Do you recognize the tune? _____

11. What term describes the wordless singing heard at the opening of this song? _____

12. How is the composer able to create emotional intensity in *Sometimes I Feel Like a Motherless Child?* _____
_____

---

90. *Review* American Musical Theater
Chap. 78 Chr/Std; 69 Sh

Exercises

Fill in the information below.

1. From which European stage genre did musical theater develop?

   _____

2. Name a popular musical from the 1920s: _____

   from the 1930s: _____

   from the 1940s: _____

   from the 1950s: _____

3. List three musicals with a literary basis and name the source for each.

   MUSICAL   BASIS

   _____   _____

   _____   _____

   _____   _____

4. Name two famous Broadway musical composer/songwriter teams and a
   show by each.

   COMPOSER/LYRICIST   SHOW

   _____   _____

   _____   _____

Match the following well-known musicals with their writers. You may use a
composer more than once.

_____   5. *Into the Woods*   a. Stephen Sondheim

_____   6. *Les Misérables*   b. Andrew Lloyd Webber

_____   7. *Evita*   c. Claude-Michel Schonberg

_____   8. *Jesus Christ Superstar*

_____   9. *Cats*

_____ 10. *Phantom of the Opera*

_____ 11. *Miss Saigon*

_____ 12. *Sweeney Todd*

13. Name several classical musicals that have recently been revived on Broadway. _____

14. Name a musical that has a tragic ending. _____

15. Name a classic musical that deals with African-American life and uses folk elements. _____

16. When was the first rock musical written? _____

    What was it? _____

    What are some others? _____

    _____

17. Name two new musicals produced by the Disney studio.

    _____

18. What is the basis for each of the two recent shows listed below?

    a. *Ragtime*: _____

    b. *Rent*: _____

19. List several "classic" musicals that have had recent revivals.

    _____

    _____

20. List three shows that you have seen (on stage or on video). Give the composer and lyricist, if you know them.

    a. _____

    b. _____

    c. _____

21. Recent musicals have been written on such literary classics as *Les Misérables* and *The Phantom of the Opera*. Suggest a book that you think could be adapted for the musical theater stage, and tell why you believe it could succeed.

    _____

    _____

    _____

    _____

    _____

    _____

91. *Listen* Bernstein's *West Side Story*
Bernstein: *West Side Story*, excerpts (**LG** 79 Chr/Std; 45 Sh; *e***LG**)

Exercises

Listen to excerpts from Bernstein's *West Side Story* while following the
Listening Guide, then answer the questions below.

1. Who wrote the lyrics to *West Side Story?* _____

2. What is the story about? _____

   _____

   What is its basis? _____

3. What gives the Mambo in *West Side Story* its Latin-American flavor?

   _____

   What gives it a jazz-like character? _____

   _____

4. What is the structure of the ballad *Tonight?* _____

   Can you hear the sections? _____

5. How is the *Tonight* ensemble like an operatic ensemble number?

   _____

   _____

   _____

6. How are the music and story of *West Side Story* still relevant today?

   _____

   _____

   _____

ABOUT THE COMPOSER

7. Is Bernstein a classical (art) or popular composer? Explain your response.

   _____

   _____

   _____

8. In addition to composing, what other musical roles did Bernstein fill
   during his lifetime? _____

   _____

   _____

92. *Explore* **Dance Music from Latin America and the Caribbean**

CP 20 Chr/Sh/Std

Exercises

Complete the following questions.

1. Name some Latin-American dances that have become popular in Europe and America, and identify their countries of origin.

_____

_____

_____

2. What are the two meanings of the word "conga"? _____

_____

_____

3. To what musical style does the term "salsa" refer? _____

_____

_____

What does the term mean literally? _____

4. What was the setting (country, city, era) for the 1999 film *Buena Vista Social Club?* _____

_____

5. Name several of the musicians who have achieved fame from this film and who have recorded solo albums. _____

_____

6. Where did ska and reggae originate? _____

Describe the musical style of ska. _____

_____

_____

Which pop song introduced the style into the United States?

_____

5. Describe the musical characteristics of reggae. _____

_____

_____

Listening Assignment:

Listen to a recording of reggae music (Bob Marley and the Wailers or any other group) or a more modern ska group and answer the questions below regarding the musical style.

Or visit the Web site (www.wwnorton.com/enjoy), read the Cultural Perspective, and choose a group to hear through the Web links.

Selection: _____

Group/Performer: _____

Melodic and rhythmic characteristics: _____

_____

_____

_____

Harmonic and formal characteristics: _____

_____

_____

Instruments used: _____

_____

_____

_____

Subject of text: _____

_____

_____

Comments: _____

_____

_____

_____

_____

_____

_____

_____

_____

---

93. *Review* **A History of Rock**
Chap. 79 Chr/Std; 70 Sh

Exercises

Complete the following questions.

1. What is rhythm and blues? _____

   Name several performers in this style. _____

   _____

2. What other styles of music contributed to the development of rock and

   roll? _____

3. Name two African-American and two white rock-and-roll stars from the
   1950s.

   African American: _____

   White: _____

4. Describe briefly each of the following popular styles, and name at least
   one performer or group associated with each.

   a. Soft rock: _____

      Group: _____

   b. Acid rock: _____

      Group: _____

   c. Art rock: _____

      Group: _____

   d. Heavy metal: _____

      Group: _____

   e. Punk rock: _____

      Group: _____

   f. Reggae: _____

      Group: _____

   g. Rap: _____

      Group: _____

   h. Grunge rock: _____

      Group: _____

5. Why are the Beatles so important to the history of rock? _____

   _____

   What accounts for their continued popularity? _____

   _____

6. How did rock videos and MTV change the way people listen to and judge popular music? _____

   _____

7. What other technological developments have revolutionized rock?

   _____

   _____

8. What two groups or performers from the 1980s do you think were the most influential to the development of rock? _____

   _____

9. What "classic" rock groups have had successful revivals? _____

   _____

   _____

10. What groups that are currently popular do you think will be remembered ten years from now? _____

    _____

    _____

11. How has the role of women in popular music changed recently?

    _____

    _____

12. Where did country/western music originate? _____

    _____

13. What instruments are typically in bluegrass? _____

    _____

14. Name several "classic" country/western performers. _____

    _____

15. Name several musicians currently popular on the country/western scene:

    _____

---

94. *Listen* The Global Scene

Think of Me, by Beau Soleil (**LG** 80 Chr/Std; 46 Sh; *e***LG**)
*Kangivumanga, by Ladysmith Black Mambazo (**LG** 81 Chr/Std; *e***LG**)

Exercises

Listen to the Beau Soleil performance of the Cuban dance *Think of Me* while following the Listening Guide, then answer questions 1–6.

1. In what part of the United States did Cajun music originate?

   _____ What are the cultural roots of the

   Cajuns? _____

2. What instruments are typically heard in Cajun dance music?

   _____

   _____

3. What are some of the special effects heard in this recording?

   _____

   _____

4. What term best describes the texture heard in *Think of Me?*

   _____

5. In which language is the text of *Think of Me?* _____

6. What musical characteristics give this dance a sense of regularity?

   _____

   What makes it complex? _____

   _____

*Listen to the Ladysmith Black Mambazo performance of *Kangivumanga* while following the Listening Guide, then answer questions 7–14.

7. What type of ensemble is this? _____

   Who is the leader? _____

8. Describe the singing style heard in this song. _____

   _____

   _____

9. What elements of this style have traditional African roots?

_____

_____

Which African tribe developed this style?_____

10. What sounds Western about this song? _____

_____

11. For what historical occasion was *Kangivumanga* written?

_____

_____

12. Describe the message presented by the text. _____

_____

_____

13. How long has this particular style been popular in the West?

_____ What group and song introduced it?

_____

14. How did Paul Simon help promote the music of South Africa?

_____

_____

95. *Explore* The International Sound
CP 21 Chr/Sh/Std

Exercises

Complete the following questions.

1. What types of international or world music CDs might you find at the music store? _____

   _____

   _____

2. Name several factors that have contributed to Americans' interest in international music. _____

   _____

   _____

   _____

3. Describe the international music influences in the recordings made by cellist Yo-Yo Ma. _____

   _____

   _____

   _____

   _____

4. Who might make field recordings in order to study and preserve traditional musics? _____

   Where might you find these recordings? _____

5. Does the world music we listen to today reflect these historical field recordings or is it more a fusion of styles? _____

   _____

   Why do you think this is so? _____

   _____

   _____

Listening Assignment

Find a recording in your college, university, or public library that represents a modern international group. Now try to locate a field recording (try Nonesuch, Explorer, or Folkways labels in your school's library) that reflects a more traditional style of performance from this culture, and compare the two. (Note the suggestions in the Cultural Perspective.)

Or visit the Web site (www.wwnorton.com/enjoy), read the Cultural Perspective, and choose a group to hear through the Web links.

Group/Performer: _____

Medium (voices/instruments) _____

Selection: _____

Describe the traditional, or folk, music on the recording you found.

_____

_____

_____

_____

_____

What elements in the popular recording are drawn from the traditional

performance you found? _____

_____

_____

_____

_____

Comments: _____

_____

_____

_____

_____

_____

_____

_____

96. *Review* The New Music
Chaps. 80–82 Chr/Std; 71–72 Sh

Exercises

Complete the following questions.

1. Name an artist associated with each of the following trends.

   a. Pop Art: _____

   b. Post-Modernism: _____

   c. Abstract Expressionism: _____

   d. New wave cinema: _____

   e. Performance art: _____

   f. Feminist art: _____

   g. Ethnic art: _____

2. List one or more major figures of the second half of the twentieth century in each discipline below; if possible, cite a work by each.

   a. Poem: _____

   _____

   b. Stage work: _____

   _____

   c. Novel: _____

   _____

   d. Film: _____

   _____

True or False

_____ 3. Total serialism is an extension of twelve-tone music to include the complex organization of other musical elements.

_____ 4. Aleatoric music refers to an ultrarational, total serial music.

_____ 5. Open form is a flexible structure related to aleatoric music.

_____ 6. John Cage was associated with aleatoric music.

_____ 7. The piano is not capable of playing microtones, because they fall between its notes.

_____ 8. Western composers have been influenced by the tuning systems and instruments of various Asian cultures.

Match the following contemporary composers with their native countries. You may use an answer more than once.

_____ 9. Pierre Boulez

_____ 10. Luciano Berio

_____ 11. Iannis Xenakis

_____ 12. Krzysztof Penderecki

_____ 13. George Perle

_____ 14. Sofia Gubaidulina

_____ 15. György Ligeti

_____ 16. George Crumb

a. Poland

b. Russia

c. Hungary

d. France

e. Italy

f. Greece

g. United States

17. Name two female virtuoso singers who have specialized in contemporary music. _____

_____

18. What kind of unusual techniques have they specialized in?

_____

_____

19. The roles of women in music, especially as composers, have changed radically over the centuries. What general perception do you have of the roles of women in classical music today?

_____

_____

_____

_____

_____

97. *Explore* Canada's Vision for a Global Culture
CP 22 Chr/Sh/Std

Exercises

Complete the following questions.

1. What cultures make up Canada's multi-ethnic population?

_____

_____

2. Name several important music institutions in Canada.

_____

3. Describe Canada's commitment to avant-garde music.

_____

_____

_____

_____

_____

4. Which contemporary Canadian writer influenced modern composers?

_____

Describe this writer's philosophy about communication in the twentieth

century. _____

_____

_____

_____

5. What is the goal of composer R. Murray Schafer's World Soundscapes

project? _____

_____

_____

6. How has Schafer changed music performance conventions?

_____

_____

_____

Listening Assignment

Investigate a multi-media or a performance art work by one of the composers listed below. Read about the work, listen to it (if possible), and discuss how it changes standard conventions of performance.

  Laurie Anderson
  John Cage
  Pauline Oliveros
  R. Murray Schafer

Or visit the Web site (www.wwnorton.com/enjoy), read the Cultural Perspective, and choose an example to hear through the Web links.

Work: _____ Date: _____

Composer: _____

Medium (performance forces): _____

_____

Description of work: _____

_____

_____

_____

_____

How does performing this work differ from standard performance rituals?

_____

_____

_____

_____

_____

Comments: _____

_____

_____

_____

_____

_____

> ### 98. *Listen* Messiaen and Boulez
> *Messiaen: *Vocalise* from *Quartet for the End of Time* (**LG** 82 Chr/Std; *e***LG**)
> *Boulez: *The Hammer Without a Master*, Nos. 1, 3, 7 (**LG** 83 Chr/Std; *e***LG**)

Exercises

*Listen to the *Vocalise* from Messiaen's *Quartet for the End of Time* while following the Listening Guide, then answer questions 1–5.

1. Where and under what circumstances was this work written?

   _____

2. What is its instrumentation? _____

   Where was it premiered? _____

3. What biblical passage inspired this quartet? _____

   What is the passage about? _____

   _____

4. In the *Vocalise for the Angel Who Announced the End of Time*, how do the

   music at the opening and closing evoke the program? _____

   _____

   What makes the middle section sound angelic? _____

   _____

5. What are some of the influences on Messiaen's music other than the

   circumstances surrounding the *Quartet for the End of Time*? _____

   _____

   _____

*Listen to the three movements from Boulez's *Hammer Without a Master* while following the Listening Guide, then answer questions 6–12.

6. What is the medium for this chamber work? _____

   _____

7. Who is the poet? _____ What is the text of No. 3

   about? _____

8. How does Boulez achieve some effects from non-Western music?

   _____

   _____

9. How would you describe the harmonic style? _____

10. What unifies this song cycle? _____

11. Describe the style of the vocal line. _____
_____

12. What important musical positions has Pierre Boulez held?

_____

_____

_____

99. *Listen* Crumb, Cage, and Ligeti

Crumb: *Ancient Voices of Children*, First Movement (**LG** 84 Chr/Std; 47 Sh; *e***LG**)
*Cage: Sonata V, from *Sonatas and Interludes* (**LG** 85 Chr/Std; *e***LG**)
Ligeti: *Disorder*, from *Etudes for Piano*, Book I (**LG** 87 Chr/Std; 48 Sh; *e***LG**)

Exercises

*Listen to Cage's Sonata V from *Sonatas and Interludes* while following the Listening Guide, then answer questions 1–5.

1. What is the overall structure of Cage's *Sonatas and Interludes*?

_____

_____

2. What is the form of Sonata V? _____

3. What is a prepared piano? _____

_____

4. What musical influence led Cage to develop the prepared piano?

_____

_____

5. Describe the timbre in your own words. _____

_____

_____

Listen to *The Little Boy Is Looking for His Voice* from Crumb's *Ancient Voices of Children* while following the Listening Guide, then answer questions 6–14.

6. Whose poetry is set in this song cycle? _____

7. What other works did Crumb set to texts by the same poet?

_____

8. What is unusual about the instruments used in this work?

_____

9. What unusual effects is the voice asked to reproduce?

_____

10. Describe the vocalise singing style that opens this song:

_____

_____

11. Can you hear when the text is finally sung? _____

12. Who sings the second strophe of the song? _____

What is unusual about the way this is sung? _____

_____

13. What non-Western styles are suggested in this song? _____

_____

14. What extraordinary singer recorded this work? _____

Listen to *Disorder* from Ligeti's *Etudes for Piano,* Book I, while following the Listening Guide, then answer questions 15–21.

15. What were some of the influences on Ligeti in writing these études?

_____

_____

16. What element is manipulated the most in this work? _____

17. Why is the title *Disorder* appropriate for this work?

_____

_____

18. How would you describe the character of this piano work?

_____

19. How does the étude end? _____

_____

20. How demanding do you think this work is to perform?

_____

21. What famous film made use of Ligeti's music? _____

What works were included in this soundtrack?_____

_____

Have you seen this film? _____

When was it made? _____

Who was the film's director? _____

---

100. *Listen* **World Music: The Sounds of Java and Eastern Africa**
*Javanese Gamelan Music: *Patalon* (**LG** 86 Chr/Std; *e***LG**)
East African Drumming: *Ensiraba ya munange Katego* (**LG** 88 Chr/Std; 49 Sh; *e***LG**)

Exercises

*Listen to *Patalon,* the Javanese gamelan selection on your recordings, while
following the Listening Guide, then answer questions 1–6.

1. What is a gamelan? _____

_____

In which cultures is this ensemble used? _____

For what types of events is it used? _____

2. What is the story told in the play from which the *Patalon* comes?

_____

_____

_____

What is the basis for this story? _____

3. What function does the *Patalon* play for the entire drama? _____

_____

4. What type of scale is featured in this work? _____

5. Describe what distinguishes the different sections of the work.

_____

_____

Can you hear the distinct sections and changes in timbre? _____

6. Of the composers we studied, which was (were) particularly influenced
by the sound of the gamelan?

_____

Listen to the selection of Ugandan drumming, *Ensiraba ya munange Katego,*
while following the Listening Guide, then answer questions 7–18.

7. Name an instrument in each category below that is played in Eastern

Africa.

Chordophone: _____

Idiophone: _____

Aerophone: _____

Membranophone: _____

8. What is an entenga ensemble? _____

9. How many players participate? _____ On how many drums? _____

10. How many drums (and pitches) does each melody drummer play? _____

11. What is the story told by this piece? _____

_____

_____

12. When the players begin, only rhythmic clicking is heard. Why?

_____

_____

13. How many different rhythmic patterns are actually played? _____

14. Can you hear the interlocking patterns and resulting complexity once
    the drummers move their strokes to the heads? _____

15. How did entenga players learn their parts in such a piece?

_____

_____

16. Which contemporary composer that we studied was influenced by this
    style of music? _____

17. Can you hear any relationship between this African drumming selection
    and the piano étude *Disorder*? _____
    Explain. _____

_____

18. How does the level of rhythmic complexity in this piece compare with
    rhythmic elements of Classical-era music (of Mozart, for example)?

_____

_____

_____

With early twentieth-century music (of Stravinsky or Bartók, for example)?

_____

_____

---

101. *Listen* **World Music: Chinese Traditional Music**
Abing: *The Moon Reflected on the Second Springs* (**LG** 89 Chr/Std; 50 Sh; *e***LG**)

Exercises

Listen to the Chinese traditional selection *The Moon Reflected on the Second Springs* while following the Listening Guide, then answer the questions below.

1. Which Chinese musician composed and first performed this work?

_____

2. Which region of China is he from? _____

3. Describe this musician's life. _____

_____

_____

_____

4. The musician was a Daoist; what does this mean?

_____

5. Why do we consider this "composed" work as traditional music?

_____

_____

6. For what instrument was *The Moon Reflected on the Second Springs*

   conceived? _____ Describe the instrument.

_____

7. What additional instrument is heard on our recording?

   _____ Describe this instrument.

_____

8. What type of scale is this work based on? _____

9. What are the pitches?_____

10. How many phrases make up the melody of this work?_____

   Are they symmetrical in length?_____

11. What does "jia hua" mean? _____

    How does the technique sound musically? _____

    _____

12. How many times is the complete melody played? _____

    Can you hear when it repeats? _____

13. Describe the sound of the erhu in your own words. Compare it with

    the Western violin. _____

    _____

    _____

    _____

    _____

    _____

14. Describe how the yangqin sounds and what role it serves in this

    performance. _____

    _____

    _____

    _____

15. Where does this performance reach its climax?

    _____

16. In your opinion, is this performance effective? _____

    Why or why not? _____

    _____

    _____

102. *Review* Music for Films
Chap. 83 Chr/Std; 73 Sh

Exercises

Complete the following questions.

  1. Describe an example in which music establishes the mood in a film.

    _____

    _____

  2. Describe an example in which music helps establish a character.

    _____

  3. Describe how music can help give a sense of place and time in a film.

    _____

  4. What does "running counter to the action" mean? _____

    _____

  5. What is the difference between "underscoring" and "source music"?

    _____

    _____

    _____

  6. What is a leitmotif? _____

    Name a film in which a leitmotif is integral to the soundtrack.

    _____

  7. How was music provided for silent films?_____

    _____

  8. What was the first "talkie," or film with a soundtrack? _____

    _____ When was it issued? _____

  9. Name a film for which each of these composers wrote the music.

    a. Max Steiner: _____

    b. Erich Wolfgang Korngold: _____

    c. Bernard Herrmann: _____

    d. Miklós Rózsa:_____

    Do you know any of these films? _____

10. What were Prokofiev's two great epic film scores?

_____

_____

11. Name an American art music composer who also wrote music for several Oscar-nominated films? _____

12. Which films with music by John Williams have you seen?

_____

_____

With music by James Horner? _____

13. Name a popular film with music by Danny Elfman.

_____

With music by Hans Zimmer: _____

14. Do you feel that any of the above composers has a recognizable style?

_____ Explain. _____

_____

_____

Match the following composers with their film scores.

_____ 15. Elmer Bernstein   a. *Crouching Tiger, Hidden Dragon*

_____ 16. Jerry Goldsmith   b. *The Truman Show*

_____ 17. Rachel Portman   c. *The Red Violin*

_____ 18. Philip Glass   d. *The Cider House Rules*

_____ 19. John Corigliano   e. *The Mummy*

_____ 20. Tan Dun   f. *Wild, Wild West*

Which of these films have you seen? _____

_____

---

103. *Listen Alexander Nevsky* **and** *Crouching Tiger, Hidden Dragon*
*Prokofiev: *Alexander Nevsky*, Seventh Movement (**LG** 90 Chr/Std; *e***LG**)
Tan Dun: *Farewell* from *Crouching Tiger, Hidden Dragon* (**LG** 91 Chr/Std; 51 Sh; *e***LG**)

Exercises

*Listen to the excerpt from *Alexander Nevsky* while following the Listening Guide, then answer questions 1–8.

1. What is the basis for the story of *Alexander Nevsky?*

_____

2. Who directed the film for which this music was originally written?

_____ When was the film made?

_____ When was this music reworked into a cantata?

_____

3. How did the film *Alexander Nevsky* and its music serve to bolster the

morale of the Russians? _____

_____

4. What aspects of the last movement of the cantata *Alexander Nevsky*

sound particularly Russian? _____

_____

Can you follow the Russian text in the Listening Guide? _____

ABOUT THE COMPOSER

5. What political pressures did Prokofiev run up against in his career?

_____

_____

6. What elements of Classicism are heard in Prokofiev's music?

_____

7. Through which elements did he strive for innovation?

_____

8. Name several well-known works by Prokofiev. _____

_____

Listen to Tan Dun's *Farewell* from *Crouching Tiger, Hidden Dragon* while following the Listening Guide, then answer questions 9–15.

9. What genre of film is *Crouching Tiger, Hidden Dragon?* _____

   Have you seen this film? _____

10. What are the principal instruments heard in the selection *Farewell?*

   _____

11. What is the formal procedure heard in *Farewell?*

   _____

12. What does the principal theme represent in the film?

   _____

13. What famous musician performs in this film score? _____

14. Name some other works by Tan Dun. _____

   _____

   _____

15. What sounds Western about this musical selection? _____

   _____

16. What sounds Chinese about the selection? _____

   _____

---

104. *Review* Technology and Music
Chap. 84 Chr/Std; 74 Sh

Exercises

Complete the following questions.

1. What is a *musique concrète?* _____

   When and where did it emerge? _____

   Name several composers associated with this trend. _____

   _____

2. How did the German *electronische Musik* differ from *musique concrète?*

   _____

3. What are some of the ways that composers manipulated tape in the
   early days of electronic music? _____

   _____

4. Name an electronic music work by the German composer Karlheinz
   Stockhausen. _____

5. What device was at the heart of the German electronic music studio?

   _____ What did it do? _____

   How was it important to later developments in electronic music?

   _____

6. The _____ was the first completely integrated
   music synthesizer. Why did so few composers have a chance to use it?

   _____

7. Who is credited with the creation of compact, affordable synthesizers?

   _____

8. Which best-selling synthesizer employed the then-new FM synthesis
   technology? _____

9. What is MIDI? _____

   _____

10. How did the development of digital sampling synthesizers advance
    musical composition? _____

    _____

Match the composers with their descriptions.

_____ 11. Edgard Varèse

a. composed *Poème électronique* for a sound and light show at the World's Fair in Brussels

_____ 12. Mario Davidovsky

b. founded the San Francisco tape center; composed *Sonic Meditations*

_____ 13. Milton Babbit

c. wrote works for tape and live performer, such as *Synchronisms*

_____ 14. Pauline Oliveros

d. composed *Philomel* and *Philonema* at the Columbia-Princeton Electronic Music Center

_____ 15. Tod Machover

e. composer/creator of the interactive installation *Brain Opera*

Listen to the excerpt from Lansky's *Notjustmoreidlechatter* (**LG** 92 Chr/Std; 52 Sh; *e***LG**) while following the Listening Guide, then answer questions 16–20.

16. What compositional methods did Paul Lansky explore in this work?

_____

_____

17. Through which technique did Lansky manipulate the sound of the human voice? _____

_____

18. Describe the "words" you hear in *Notjustmoreidlechatter*.

_____

_____

19. Do you hear the chord progression under the "voices"? _____

Do you sense the returns to the opening chords? _____

20. What is your reaction to this piece? _____

_____

_____

105. *Explore* Artificial Intelligence: The Composer's New Tool
CP 23 Chr/Sh/Std

Exercises

Complete the following.

1. Who is considered the world's first computer programmer?

   _____ What did she conceive of

   that was far ahead of her time? _____

2. The first AI programs that were used to compose music depended on

   _____ in the form of rules.

3. What were the capabilities of David Cope's AI program called Experiments

   in Musical Intelligence? _____

   _____

4. What new methods of AI have emerged in recent years? _____

   _____

   _____

5. How do genetic algorithms work? _____

   _____

6. Why are neural networks a valuable tool for composers, music theorists,

   and musicologists? _____

   _____

7. What recent methodology allows the computer to solve problems (such

   as creating a melody)? _____

8. Besides melody, what aspects of a composition can emerge from the

   evolutionary process of genetic algorithms? _____

   _____

   _____

Essay

What impact do you think AI (artificial intelligence) and music will have on future generations of professional and amateur composers? What will become of traditional composition techniques? Will there still be a need for formal musical training?

Or visit the Web site (www.wwnorton.com/enjoy), read the Cultural Perspective, then follow the Web links to discover more about AI and music. Summarize your findings below.

---

106. *Review* New Romanticism and Minimalism
Chap. 85 Chr/Std; 75 Sh

Exercises

Multiple Choice

_____ 1. Which of the following best sums up the aspirations of composers
of the New Romanticism?
  a. purely intellectual, completely serial composition
  b. music as "the language of the emotions"
  c. formal, constructivist art

_____ 2. The New Romantics sought to:
  a. close the gap between composers and listeners.
  b. further widen the gap between composers and listeners.
  c. follow the harmonic and melodic language of the Baroque.

Complete the following questions.

3. Name three composers who are advocates of the New Romanticism.

_____

_____

4. Who was the first woman to win a Pulitzer Prize in composition?

_____

5. Which composer has written several works to commemorate AIDS

victims? _____ Name one of the

works. _____

6. Which composer's music is centered around nature and water?

_____ Name a work that illustrates

this theme. _____

Multiple Choice

_____ 7. Which term best describes the marked stylistic feature of
minimalist music?
  a. dissonance
  b. repetition
  c. contrast

_____ 8. What was the primary impetus for minimalist composers?
  a. a return to simplicity
  b. a total abandonment of form
  c. a desire for overstatement

9. Name three composers who are considered minimalists. _____

_____

_____

10. How would you describe the effect that minimalist music has on the listener? _____

_____

11. 3. Name two operas by John Adams and tell the historical event that spawned each. _____

_____

12. Which style do you think will last longer, New Romanticism or minimalism? _____ Why? _____

_____

_____

13. What is spiritual minimalism? _____

_____

Name three composers who are considered spiritual minimalists.

_____

_____

14. During which famous historical event of 1997 was a spiritual minimalist work featured? _____

Which work? _____

---

107. *Listen* Today's Composers: Tower, Pärt, and Adams
Tower: *For the Uncommon Woman* (**LG** 93 Chr/Std; 53 Sh; *e***LG**)
Pärt: *Cantate Domino canticum novum* (**LG** 94 Chr/Std; 54 Sh; *e***LG**)
Adams *Roadrunner,* from *Chamber Symphony* (**LG** 95 Chr/Std; 55 Sh; *e***LG**)

Exercises

Listen to Joan Tower's *For the Uncommon Woman* while following the Listening Guide, then answer questions 1–5.

1. 1. Which composer inspired the first of Tower's *Fanfares for the*

   Uncommon Woman? _____

2. To whom does the series of fanfares pay homage? _____

   _____

3. What instrument families are prominently heard in *For the Uncommon*

   Woman? _____

4. How would you describe the harmony heard in this work? _____

   _____

5. In your opinion, what, if anything, is "Romantic" about this work?

   _____

   _____

Listen to Arvo Pärt's *Cantate Domino canticum novum* while following the Listening Guide, then answer questions 6–11.

6. Where was the composer Arvo Pärt born? _____

7. How have the composer's religious beliefs influenced his compositions?

   _____

   _____

8. What is the source of the text for *Cantate Domino?* _____

   In what language is it sung? _____

   _____

9. How would you describe the texture of this work? _____

   _____

10. How does Pärt achieve the unique tintinnabular style in this work?

    _____

11. Can this work, and Pärt's style in general, be viewed as minimalist? _____

   If so, how? _____

   _____

Listen to the third movement of Adams's *Chamber Symphony* while following the Listening Guide, then answer questions 12–16.

12. 1. What was the inspiration for the third movement, *Roadrunner*?

   _____

   _____

13. What nontraditional instrument plays a key role in this work?

   _____

14. How would you describe Adams's treatment of rhythm in this movement?

   _____

   _____

15. How would you describe the role of the solo violin in this movement?

   _____

   _____

16. In what way could *Roadrunner* be viewed as minimalist in style? _____

   As Romantic in style? _____

   _____

108. *Review* Music Notation
Appendix I

Exercises

Answer the following questions about the musical example below. The piece is a Jamaican folk song entitled *Matilda*.

Ma - til - da,____ Ma - til - da,____ Ma - til - da, she take me mon - ey

run Ve-ne-zue-la____

1. The clef sign used is called a(n) _____.

2. The first three pitches are _____, _____, and _____.

3. The time signature indicates a duple meter known as cut time and

   means the same as 2/2. This means that a _____ note gets one beat,

   with _____ beats per measure.

4. The first note indicates a dotted _____ note.

5. What does a dot do to the rhythmic value of a note?

   _____

6. The curved line connecting notes of the same pitch is called a

   _____.

7. What rhythmic technique is used to throw off the meter by temporarily

   shifting the accent? _____

8. To what extent does this example use this technique?

   ___ a lot   ___ somewhat   ___ a little

9. In this meter, how many eighth notes make up one beat?

   _____ How many quarter notes? _____

10. How many measures are there in this example? _____

11. Measures 3 and 4 outline a triad beginning on _____.

12. Measures 5 and 6 outline a triad beginning on _____.

13. What key is this example in? _____ How do you know?

   _____

14. Name a song you know that begins with an upbeat.

   _____

15. Name a song you know that is in triple meter.

   _____

16. What is the sign for a sharp? _____

   What is its function? _____

17. What is the sign for a flat? _____

   What is its function? _____

18. How do you cancel a flat or sharp? _____

19. What is the function of a key signature? _____

   _____

20. Does the song *Matilda* reproduced above have a key signature? _____

21. How do you show a quarter-note rest? _____

22. What is the most common compound meter? _____

   Name a song in compound meter. _____

23. What do you call short lines above or below the staff on which pitches
   are written? _____

24. How many thirty-second notes make up a half note? _____

25. How many sixteenth notes are in a whole note? _____

26. Write a melody on the staff below, beginning with a clef, time signature,
   and key signature. You can make up the pitches and rhythms, but make
   sure your rhythmic notation is correct for each measure.

WORKBOOK ACTIVITIES

The following exercises allow you to explore various types of music on your own or with a small group (a study or discussion group, for example). They are designed to make you more aware of the diverse opportunities you have to hear music and to participate actively in making music. These exercises are meant to guide you in doing special projects and in completing work assigned by your instructor. The activities can, of course, be varied, and there are many others that could be educational. If you have ideas for projects, talk them over with your instructor.

Activity 1: Keep a Music Journal

Goal: To become more aware of music in your environment.

For four days, keep a journal in the space below, noting all the instances in which you listen to or hear music, whether by your own choosing or by accident. Consider the following in your journal: your clock-radio, car and/or home stereo, television (even as background music), work environment, class, stores, and elevators.

Day 1: Date _____

AM: _____

_____

_____

_____

PM: _____

_____

_____

_____

_____

Day 2: Date _____

AM: _____

_____

_____

_____

PM: _____

_____

_____

_____

_____

Day 3: Date _____

AM: _____

_____

_____

_____

PM: _____

_____

_____

_____

_____

Day 4: Date _____

AM: _____

_____

_____

_____

PM: _____

_____

_____

_____

_____

Were you surprised how often (or seldom) you heard music?

_____

Were you more aware than usual of music in your environment? _____

Was any of the music distracting or annoying? _____

Comments: _____

_____

_____

_____

_____

Activity 2: Interview a Musician

Goal: To gain insight into musical performance from an active participant.

Find a musician—performer or conductor—on campus (a music student or an instructor) and arrange an interview. Ask the musician the questions below, along with others that you supply.

Interview Questions

What is your name? _____

Are you _____ a performer, _____ a conductor, or _____ both?

How long have you studied music? _____

What instrument(s) do you play? _____

Do you sing? _____ If yes, what voice range? _____

In which music ensembles have you participated and in what capacity?

_____

_____

_____

Do you take part in concerts frequently? _____

Approximately how many performances a year? _____

Describe a recent performance in which you participated (group, which instrument/voice, and repertory performed).

_____

_____

_____

_____

_____

How is active participation in music making different from passive listening?

_____

_____

_____

_____

What decisions must you make while performing music?

_____

_____

_____

_____

What styles of music do you most often perform?

____ classical   ____ popular   ____ traditional

Describe the specific styles you perform frequently.

_____

_____

Do you now (or plan to) make your living as a musician? ____ yes ____ no

Comments: _____

What are the advantages of a career in music? _____

_____

_____

What are the disadvantages? _____

_____

_____

(Your comments here): _____

_____

_____

_____

_____

Activity 3: Interview an International Student

Goal: To learn about the music of another culture from a native of the culture.

Find an international student or instructor on your campus. (Ask in your classes, post a note on a dorm or student union bulletin board, or ask at the International Office on your campus.) Arrange to meet with this person and ask the questions below, along with others that you supply.

Interview Questions

What is your name? _____

What country do you come from? _____

What is your native language? _____

How long have you been in this country? _____

What are you studying here? _____

Have you ever studied music? _____

Do you play any instruments? _____ If yes, which one(s)?

_____

Did you learn any native folk songs as a child? _____

Can you sing or play one, or tell me about one?

Title: _____ Language: _____

What is it about? _____

_____

_____

(To the interviewer: make your own notes about the song below.)

_____

_____

What kind of instruments are used in your native folk music?

_____

What roles does music play in your society? _____

_____

Do women study music there? If so, what kind? _____

_____

223

Do men study music there? If so, what kind? _____

_____

What kind of music do you like to listen to? _____

_____

Do you plan to take any music classes while studying here? _____

If yes, which? _____

Have you been to any concerts in this country? _____

If yes, which? _____

_____

Is popular music in your country influenced by American popular styles?

_____ If yes, in what way? _____

_____

(Note other questions you asked below with the answers or any comments
you have about the interview.)

_____

_____

_____

_____

_____

_____

_____

_____

_____

_____

Activity 4: Experience Traditional Music

Goal: To become familiar with a traditional or folk music style, its instruments, its performers, and its performance context.

Attend a folk music session of your choice, either in an informal performance setting, such as a coffee house or a folk festival, or in a concert hall, perhaps as part of your campus's sponsored events.

Complete the questions below.

Date of event: _____ Location: _____

Title of event: _____

Performers or groups heard: _____

_____

Folk culture(s) represented: _____

_____

Which instruments were played? _____

_____

Describe the singing style (if applicable). _____

_____

Was there dancing? _____ If so, what style and dance types?

_____

_____

Were the performers in costume? _____ If so, describe the costumes.

_____

_____

Describe the performance setting and its atmosphere.

_____

_____

_____

_____

What are some of the musical characteristics of this traditional music style (consider melody, rhythm and meter, harmony, and texture)?

_____

_____

_____

_____

Try to talk with the performers during a break (at an informal event) or after the concert (musicians generally welcome questions about their performance or instruments).

How did they become interested in this particular traditional style?

_____

_____

_____

Is it part of their cultural heritage? _____

Ask about the instruments or dancing and describe their comments below.

_____

_____

_____

_____

What did you most enjoy about the event? _____

_____

Would you attend another concert like this one? _____

Activity 5: Experience an International Night Out

Goal: To hear live music from another culture, either in a concert or restaurant setting.

Attend a concert on campus or in the community by a non-Western group (solo performer, choral, instrumental, or dance group), or go to an international restaurant that features live traditional music.

Complete the questions below.

Date of event: _____ Place: _____

Was this a _____ concert or _____ restaurant entertainment?

Names of performers: _____

_____

Country or culture of origin: _____

Did you hear singing? _____ yes _____ no

If yes, describe the style you heard. _____

_____

Did you hear instruments? _____ yes _____ no

If yes, which instruments? _____

_____

Did you see dancing? _____ yes _____ no

If yes, what style of dancing was it? _____

_____

Were the performers in native costume? _____ yes _____ no

If yes, describe them. _____

_____

Do you know the titles of any works performed? _____ yes _____ no

If yes, list some. _____

_____

Describe the music you heard in your own words (consider the melody, rhythm, harmony, and texture).

_____

_____

_____

_____

_____

_____

Did you like the music? _____ yes _____ no

Why or why not? _____

_____

If you attended a restaurant, did you eat ethnic food? _____ yes _____ no

If yes, what kinds? _____

_____

Did you like the food? _____ yes _____ no

Is this the first time you have heard live music of this style? _____ yes _____ no

Would you go to another concert/restaurant entertainment of the same type?

_____ yes _____ no

Activity 6: Explore PBS Programming

Goal: To become aware of the diverse music programs and live performances available on PBS (Public Broadcasting System).

Find a TV station in your area that is affiliated with the Public Broadcasting System, and review the programming for a week. Watch any style of music program and discuss it below.

Program title: _____

Station: _____ Date/time of program: _____

Major performers/groups: _____

_____

_____

Titles of selected works (if known): _____

_____

_____

What type of music was performed?

___ classical. If yes, what eras? _____

___ popular. If yes, what styles? _____

___ traditional. If yes, what styles? _____

___ non-Western. If yes, what styles? _____

If dramatic music, was it a(n) ___ opera ___ ballet ___ musical ___ other?

List other music programs offered during the week. _____

_____

_____

_____

_____

_____

_____

Describe the performance in your own words. Try to mention some elements of musical style, and evaluate the performance.

_____

_____

_____

_____

_____

_____

_____

_____

_____

_____

_____

_____

_____

_____

Did you enjoy the program? ___ yes ___ no ___ somewhat

Would you have enjoyed it ___ more ___ less ___the same if you had been at the live performance?

Comments: _____

_____

_____

_____

_____

Activity 7: View Opera from Home

Goal: To become familiar with an opera of your choice and its characteristic traits.

Go to your local video store, or campus or public library, select an opera video that interests you, watch it, and discuss it below.

Opera title: _____

Composer: _____

When was the opera written (check your text)? _____

In what language is it sung? _____

Does the video have English subtitles? ____ yes ____ no

Which opera company performed? _____

Name the leading solo performers (check credits or box).

_____

_____

_____

Who are the main characters in the opera? _____

_____

_____

_____

Summarize the plot below. _____

_____

_____

_____

_____

_____

_____

_____

_____

_____

_____

_____

_____

_____

_____

_____

_____

Was this ___ comic or ____ serious opera?

Did it begin with an instrumental overture? ____ yes ___ no

Check below the vocal styles that you heard.

___ aria ___ recitative ___ solo ensemble ___ chorus

Describe the music in your own words. _____

_____

_____

_____

_____

_____

Did you enjoy the opera? ___ yes ___ no ___ somewhat

Would you like to see another? ___ yes ___ no

If yes, ___ on video or ___ in live performance?

Comments: _____

_____

_____

_____

_____

Activity 8: Explore a Music Video Network

Goal: To assess the programming on a music video network and the impact the network has had on popular music.

Review MTV (or another music video network) programming for two or three days, choose several diverse music programs to watch, and answer the following questions.

Name of network selected: _____

Program (1) title: _____

Date: _____ Time: _____ Program length: _____

Program (2) title: _____

Date: _____ Time: _____ Program length: _____

List some of the other programs offered that you did not select.

_____

_____

_____

Describe program 1 (groups performing, focus, or theme).

_____

_____

_____

_____

_____

_____

What styles of popular music were included?

____ soft rock   ____ punk rock

____ folk rock   ____ reggae

____ jazz rock   ____ rap

____ art rock   ____ grunge rock

____ Latin rock   ____ new wave

____ heavy metal

other _____

233

Describe one musical style you heard and its characteristics.

_____

_____

Describe program 2 (groups performing, focus, or theme).

_____

_____

_____

_____

_____

_____

What styles of popular music were included?

___ soft rock	___ punk rock
___ folk rock	___ reggae
___ jazz rock	___ rap
___ art rock	___ grunge rock
___ Latin rock	___ new wave
___ heavy metal	

other: _____

_____

Describe one musical style you heard and its characteristics.

_____

_____

Do you watch MTV or other music video network often? ___ yes ___ no
___ sometimes

Do you prefer ___ watching a video network or ___ listening to a CD or cassette?

Explain your answer. _____

_____

What effect do you think MTV and other video networks have had on the popular music industry?

_____

_____

234

Activity 9: Relive the Original Woodstock Festival, 1969

Goal: To become familiar with various 1960s-era rock groups and styles through a historic event.

Go to your college or public library or to a video store and check out the double video of the original Woodstock Festival, held in 1969. View parts of it and answer the following questions. Some recommended performances on the video with counter numbers and timings are provided for easy access.

Tape 1

Counter	Time	Performer/Group	Song
1785	23:10	Richie Havens	*Freedom* (adapted from *Motherless Child*)
2708	40:00	Joan Baez	*Joe Hill* *Swing Low, Sweet Chariot*
2965	45:25	The Who	*We're Not Gonna Take It* *Summertime Blues*
3770	63:50	Sha-Na-Na	*At the Hop*
3978	68:40	Joe Cocker	*With a Little Help from My Friends*

Tape 2

Counter	Time	Performer/Group	Song
0000	0:00	Country Joe and the Fish	*Rock and Soul Music*
0225	3:30	Arlo Guthrie	*Comin' into Los Angeles*
0580	6:15	Crosby, Stills and Nash	*Judy Blue Eyes*
1280	15:20	Ten Years After	*I'm Going Home*
2370	25:00	John Sebastian	*Rainbows All Over Your Blues*
2664	40:50	Country Joe MacDonald	*I Feel Like I'm Fixin' to Die Rag*
3185	51:37	Santana	*Soul Sacrifice*
3597	61:07	Sly and the Family Stone	*I Want to Take You Higher*
4382	81:00	Jimi Hendrix	*The Star-Spangled Banner*

Select three performances representing different groups and styles and answer the following questions.

Group (1): _____

Title (1): _____

What style of rock is this? _____

Did you know the group or recording prior to this video?

___ group ___ song ___ both

Describe the musical elements of the style. _____

_____

_____

_____

Group (2): _____

Title (2): _____

What style of rock is this? _____

Did you know the group or recording prior to this video?

___ group ___ song ___ both

Describe the musical elements of the style. _____

_____

_____

_____

Group (3): _____

Title (3): _____

What style of rock is this? _____

Did you know the group or recording prior to this video?

___ group ___ song ___ both

Describe the musical elements of the style. _____

_____

_____

_____

Why is this Woodstock Festival remembered as a historic event? _____

_____

_____

_____

Activity 10: Sing Karaoke

Goal: To be actively involved in music performance as an amateur singer.

Find a karaoke club in your area, or check out or buy a karaoke track to use at home or in class, and perform as a solo singer or with a group. (If you are unsure what karaoke is, look it up in your text.)

Date: _____ Location: _____

List the song(s) you sang: _____

_____

_____

List songs others sang: _____

_____

_____

Did you know the words for the songs you sang? ___ yes ___ no

Did you have the words available to look at? ___ yes ___ no

If yes, did you have ___ a printed text or ___ a monitor?

Did you sing ___ as a soloist or ___ with a group?

Describe how it felt to be a singer. _____

_____

_____

_____

_____

Were you able to sing in tune (on pitch)?

___ yes ___ no ___ sometimes

Do you think you have a good singing voice? ___ yes ___ no

Did other singers sing in tune?

___ yes ___ no ___ sometimes

Describe how one of the other singers sounded. _____

_____

_____

Did others have good singing voices?

___ yes ___ no ___ some did

In your opinion, what determines a good voice? _____

_____

_____

_____

Where did the tradition of karaoke singing originate?

_____

What do you think accounts for its popularity? _____

_____

_____

Have you ever done this before? ___ yes ___ no

Would you enjoy trying it again? ___ yes ___ no

Activity 11: Engage in Group Singing

Goal: To study imitation through the singing of a round.

The song below is a famous round titled *Sumer is icumen in,* or the Sumer Canon. The song is in medieval English and dates from the thirteenth century. It has a melody that can be sung as a four-voice round, with two additional lower voices singing an ostinato (called a *pes,* pronounced "pace").

Practice singing the melody line together, then learn the two lower parts. To sing as a round, divide into melody singers (four people or groups; two or three are also possible) and ostinato, or *pes,* singers (two people or groups). Have the two lower parts begin (they will help keep time), then have melody group 1 enter, then group 2, then 3, and finally 4, in overlapping imitation. Each group enters with the melody, starting when the previous group reaches number 2 in the music; each continues through the whole piece, repeating it as many times as needed. Remember that a round can go on indefinitely, so decide how many times you will sing the work.

Note that the lower parts are notated in the bass clef. (*Performance note:* The music is transposed to C major. A score of the resulting piece is on the next page. Instruments may be used instead of voices on any parts.)

Poem	*Translation (modern English)*
Sing cuccu; sing cuccu, nu	Sing cuckoo; sing cuckoo, now
Sing cuccu, nu sing cuccu!	Sing cuckoo, now sing cuckoo!
Sumer is icumen in,	Summer is coming on,
Lhude sing cuccu!	Loudly sing cuckoo!
Groweth sed and bloweth med,	The seeds are growing and the meadow is blooming,
And springth the wde nu.	And the woods are budding.
Sing cuccu!	Sing cuckoo!
Awe bleteth after lomb,	The ewe bleats for the lamb,
Lhouth after calve cu;	The cow lows for the calf;
Bulloc sterteth,	The bullock jumps,
Bucke verteth,	The buck breaks wind,
Murie sing cuccu.	Merrily sing cuckoo.
Cuccu, cuccu,	Cuckoo, cuckoo,
Wel singes thu cuccu,	Well you sing cuckoo,
Ne swik thu naver nu.	Do not ever stop now.

Melody and 2 short *pes* (ostinato) parts:

Resulting music when sung as a round, showing imitation of lines:

Activity 12: Write a Rap Song

Goal: To understand what musical elements make up rap and to recreate the style.

Create a rap song of your own composition. Since rap is a combination of rhymed lyrics spoken or recited over a rhythm track, you have two different tasks:

1. Create a rhythm track with a steady beat. You can do this in one of four ways:
   a. record simple rhythmic patterns you make up and play;
   b. produce a "sample" from sounds or older prerecorded pieces that you record;
   c. use a prerecorded rhythm setting on an electronic keyboard or drum machine; or
   d. buy a rap rhythm track in a music store.

If you write your own rhythmic accompaniment, it can be very simple. Think in terms of long (L) and short (S) durations, and make it in quadruple meter. Here is an example that should be counted in 4 at a quick pace (notice it begins with an upbeat):

SSL   SL SSL SL SSL SL
4 1 2 3 4 1 2 3 4 1 2 3

2. Write a text (text is typically rhymed) to recite over the accompanying track. Your text should be about some current issue (political, social, or environmental).

Do you listen to rap? ___ yes ___ no ___ sometimes

Which groups do you know? _____

_____

_____

_____

What is the subject matter of the rap songs you know? _____

_____

_____

_____

_____

Describe how you created a rhythm track for your song.

_____

_____

_____

_____

_____

_____

Write your song text in the space below.

_____

_____

_____

_____

_____

_____

_____

_____

_____

_____

What do you like (or dislike) about rap from a musical point of view?

_____

_____

_____

_____

_____

Activity 13: Play in a Percussion Ensemble

Goal: To understand polyrhythm through the spontaneous creation of a group rhythmic work.

Work with a small group of students (three to six), with each providing a percussion instrument of his or her choice. This instrument can be anything that produces either a definite or an indefinite pitch. Ideally, the instruments should have differing timbres.

1. Choose a master percussionist, or leader, to give signals to play and stop.

2. Choose a number to determine the overall rhythmic cycle (the example below is based on 12). Have each player determine a different pattern to play within that cycle, as in additive meters. Be sure to keep a steady beat throughout.

```
Player 1    1  2  3  4  5  6  7  8  9  10  11  12
               X     X     X  X     X     X        X

Player 2    1  2  3  4  5  6  7  8  9  10  11  12
               X  X     X  X     X  X        X   X

Player 3    1  2  3  4  5  6  7  8  9  10  11  12
               X        X        X           X

Player 4    1  2  3  4  5  6  7  8  9  10  11  12
               X  X  X     X  X  X     X   X   X
```

3. Play the piece, allowing one instrument to start, then adding others. You may wish to have one player count out loud. As the sound builds to a climax, players may decide to improvise on their patterns. Watch the master percussionist for a cue to stop. Try this several times until you are satisfied with the result, then try other patterns.

List the percussion instruments used.

Player 1: _____

Player 2: _____

Player 3: _____

Player 4: _____

Player 5: _____

Player 6: _____

Which player was designated the master percussionist? _____

4. Make a musical score by aligning the different beat patterns chosen by the performers (the grid below allows for patterns of up to 19 beats).

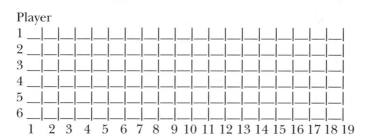

Were players successful at keeping a steady beat?

___ yes ___ no ___ somewhat

What were the difficulties in the performance? _____

_____

_____

_____

Did players freely improvise during the performance?

___ yes ___ no ___ some did

Describe how you achieved polyrhythm in your composition.

_____

_____

_____

Evaluate your musical efforts. _____

_____

_____

_____

Activity 14: Sample a Music Group on the Web

Goal: To use the web as a resource for information about a performing group, its activities, and its recordings.

Choose a current music performance group (rock, jazz, folk, or classical) that you do not know well. Using a search engine such as Yahoo, HotBot, Google, or Alta Vista, locate one or more Web sites with information on the group.

Group selected: _____

Search engine used: _____

How many sites did you find? _____

Does the group have its own official site? _____

Are there many "fan" sites for the group? _____

Peruse one or more of the sites to answer the following questions.

Who are the performers in the group? _____

_____

What instruments, if any, are included? _____

_____

What style of music does the group represent? _____

Is there historical information about the group? _____

If so, summarize its history here. _____

_____

Is there a discography provided? _____ Which recording company

issues the group's music? _____

Is there a current schedule posted for the group? _____

If so, where could you go to experience the group live? _____

Are there links provided to other related sites? _____

If so, what kind of sites are linked? _____

Is it possible to hear musical examples? _____

If so, follow the directions to hear a sample of the group's music. Which work did you select? _____

Describe the style of the work in your own words. _____

_____

_____

_____

Can you purchase recordings by the group on the same or a linked site? _____

Are you interested in hearing more music by this group? ___ yes ___ no

What do you like or dislike about the group's music? _____

_____

_____

_____

Activity 15: Sample a Modern Composer on the Web

Goal: To use the Web to "meet" a modern composer, learn of the composer's recent artistic activities, and hear a sample of music by the composer.

Find the Web site of a living composer by using a search engine, such as Yahoo, HotBot, Google, or Alta Vista. You may use a composer discussed in your text, for example, Joan Tower, Tan Dun, Andrew Lloyd Webber, or Stephen Sondheim.

Which composer did you select? _____

How did you find the Web site? _____

What is the Web address? _____

Is the site posted by _____ the composer or _____ a commercial firm?

Are there other sites for this composer? _____

If so, how many? _____

What kind of information is posted on the site you selected?

_____

_____

In which genres does this composer write? _____

_____

What are the composer's recent projects? _____

_____

_____

What composition awards has this composer won? _____

_____

Is there a discography of available recordings listed? _____

Which recording company publishes this composer's works?

_____

Is it possible to hear music examples? _____

If so, follow the directions to hear something by the composer.

What did you select? _____

247

Describe the style in your own words. _____

_____

_____

_____

What general musical style would this selection be considered?

            ____ avant-garde   ____ jazz-inspired

            ____ minimalism   ____ rock-inspired

            ____ New Romanticism   ____ musical theater

            other _____

What did you like about the sample you heard of the composer's music?

_____

_____

Would you be interested in hearing more works by this composer?

___ yes   ___ perhaps, but in a different style   ___ no

CONCERT REPORTS

The following section is designed to guide you in knowing what to listen for at concerts and how to write a concert report. Prior to going to any concerts, be sure to read pages 9–13 in your text, "Attending Concerts," to help you know what to expect, to learn traditional concert etiquette, and to assist you in finding interesting programs on your campus or in your community.

There are five concert report outlines in this section, each designed for a particular type of program. The questions vary slightly, depending on whether the works are vocal or instrumental, and popular or world music. The forms ask that you focus your attention on one or two selections to describe in some detail. Some concerts offer a mixture of styles and genres; in these cases, use either report form 1 or 2, or ask your instructor for advice. The report forms provided are:

1. Instrumental music (for orchestras, bands, chamber music, and solo recitals)
2. Choral/Vocal music (for choirs, choruses, and solo vocalists)
3. Dramatic music (for operas, musicals, and plays with music)
4. Popular music (for rock and jazz groups or soloists)
5. World music (for traditional and non-Western groups or soloists)

This section begins with a sample outline and report, based on the program reproduced on the following page. These are meant to serve as guidelines in approaching your assignment or special project. Your instructor may ask you to submit a written report only, in which case you may want to take the outline form with you to the concert and use it to jot down your own notes. Alternatively, your instructor may wish to have only the completed outline, or both the report form and a prose report. You will probably be asked to submit a copy of the concert program and perhaps to attach the canceled ticket stub. Be sure to find out what your instructor requires before completing any assignment.

PROGRAM

Overture to *A Midsummer Night's Dream*

Felix Mendelssohn
(1809–1847)

Symphony No. 41 in C major, K. 551
(*Jupiter*)
  Allegro vivace
  Andante cantabile
  Menuetto (Allegretto) & Trio
  Finale (Molto allegro)

W. A. Mozart
(1756–1791)

INTERMISSION

Concerto No. 1 for Piano and Orchestra
  in B-flat minor, Op. 23
  Allegro non troppo e molto maestoso; Allegro con spirito
  Andantino simplice; Prestissimo; Tempo I
  Allegro con fuoco

P. I. Tchaikovsky
(1840–1893)

Barbara Allen, piano

The University Symphony Orchestra
Eugene Castillo, conductor

Orchestra   ATTACH
Band   TICKET
Chamber music   STUB
Solo recital   HERE

Concert Setting

Date of concert: _March 8, 2003_

Place of concert: _Carpenter Performing Arts Center_

Name of group(s) performing: _University Symphony_
   Orchestra, Eugene Castillo, conductor

Briefly describe the concert setting (hall, performers' dress).
   the hall was large — over 1,000 seats
   performers wore black (formal dress)

Were concert programs provided? _✓_ yes ___ no. If yes, attach a copy.

Were program notes provided? _✓_ yes ___ no

Were there any spoken remarks about the concert? ___ yes _✓_ no

Could you follow the order of the concert? _✓_ yes ___ no

Were there any aspects of concert conventions that surprised you? _____

Which? _____

Concert Music

Which genres of music were performed (such as symphony or sonata)?

   overture, symphony, concerto

_____

Did you read about any of the works performed? _✓_ yes ___no

If yes, where? _✓_ program notes ___ textbook ___ outside reading

Were any of the works programmatic (with literary or pictorial associations)?

_✓_ yes ___ no

If yes, which? ___ _Overture to A Midsummer Night's Dream_ ___

What historical eras were represented on the program?

___ pre-1600   ___ Baroque _✓_ Classical _✓_ Romantic ___ 20th century

251

Choose two works from the program. Name the composer, the work, and the movement (if applicable), and compare the works in the following outline.

	FIRST WORK	SECOND WORK
Composer:	*Mendelssohn*	*Tchaikovsky*
Title:	*A Midsummer Night's Dream*	*Concerto No. 1 for Piano*
Movement or Section:	*opening*	*First*
Melody:	*high range and disjunct, later conjunct*	*wide range—sweeping*
Rhythm/ Meter:	*duple*	*triple*
Harmony:	*consonant*	*a little dissonant*
Texture:	*homophonic*	*homophonic*
Tempo:	*Allegro (very fast)*	*Allegro (fast)*
Dynamics:	*soft at opening, then grows louder*	*loud (forte) for opening—later soft*
Instruments:	*woodwinds begin, then strings, later full orchestra*	*begins with French horns, then piano and full orchestra*
Mood:	*enchanted*	*dramatic*
Other:		

What was your overall reaction to the concert?
  ✓ enjoyed it a lot   ____ enjoyed it somewhat
  ____ did not enjoy it much   ____ did not enjoy it at all

What did you like about it? *the orchestra was all students*

What did you not like about it? *noisy students in the audience*

Other comments:

Sample Report: Concert Report 1

I attended the University Symphony Orchestra concert on Saturday night, March 8. The group was made up of student musicians and was conducted by Eugene Castillo. The pianist, Barbara Allen, is a music faculty member.

The concert hall was larger than I expected—it seated over 1,000 people, and it was nearly full. I had a good seat about halfway back in the hall. The orchestra was already on stage when I arrived. When the lights went down, the first violinist stood up and signaled the oboe player to play a note to tune the orchestra. Next, the conductor entered and led the orchestra in the first work, the Overture to *A Midsummer Night's Dream* by Mendelssohn, an early Romantic composer. The notes on my program explained that this was a programmatic work based on the Shakespeare play, which I had read in high school. It was easy to follow the melodies for the different characters. The first theme was played by the strings in a high range, very lightly, reminding me of the fairies in the play. Later, the strings played a smooth, conjunct melody that was the love theme. This was followed by a humorous, disjunct theme. All these themes returned near the end of the piece. The work was in duple meter and was mostly consonant.

The next work was a symphony by Mozart, his last, according to the program. It had four movements and was written in a major key. The first movement was an Allegro in sonata-allegro form. Then came a slow movement and a triple-meter minuet. The last movement was the fastest of all, with a mostly conjunct opening melody. This work was written in the Classical era.

After the intermission, the orchestra and the soloist, Barbara Allen, played a piano concerto by the late Romantic Russian composer Tchaikovsky. This piece was long and very dramatic. The first movement had several sections. It began fast, first with the French horns, then the piano entered with disjunct chords. The strings introduced the first melody. The piano soloist played without music, and her part seemed very difficult. Her hands moved quickly as she played high and low notes on the piano. This piece was more dissonant than the other works on the program. The second movement was quiet and melancholy in mood, with a fast middle section. The last movement was in triple meter and sounded like a dance.

I enjoyed this concert very much, except for some noisy students sitting in front of me. I was impressed with how well the student musicians could play. I hope to be able to attend more concerts on campus in the future.

Concert Report 1: Instrumental Music

Orchestra   ATTACH
Band   TICKET
Chamber music   STUB
Solo recital   HERE

Concert Setting

Date of concert: _____

Place of concert: _____

Name of group(s) performing: _____

_____

Briefly describe the concert setting (hall, performers' dress):

_____

_____

Were concert programs provided? ___ yes ___ no If yes, attach a copy.

Were program notes provided? ___ yes ___ no

Were there any spoken remarks about the concert? ___ yes ___ no

Could you follow the order of the concert? ___ yes ___ no

Were there any aspects of concert conventions that surprised you? _____

Which? _____

Concert Music

Which genres of music were performed (such as symphony or sonata)?

_____

_____

Did you read about any of the works performed? ___ yes ___ no

If yes, where? ___ program notes ___ textbook ___ outside reading

Were any of the works programmatic (with literary or pictorial

associations)? ___ yes ___ no

If yes, which? _____

What historical eras were represented on the program?

___ pre-1600 ___ Baroque ___ Classical ___ Romantic ___ 20th century

255

Choose two works from the program. Name the composer, the work, and the movement (if applicable) and compare the works in the following outline:

	FIRST WORK	SECOND WORK
Composer:	_____	_____
Title:	_____	_____
Movement or Section:	_____	_____
Melody:	_____	_____
	_____	_____
Rhythm/ Meter:	_____	_____
Harmony:	_____	_____
	_____	_____
Texture:	_____	_____
	_____	_____
Tempo:	_____	_____
	_____	_____
Dynamics:	_____	_____
	_____	_____
Instruments:	_____	_____
	_____	_____
Mood:	_____	_____
Other:	_____	_____

What was your overall reaction to the concert?
___ enjoyed it a lot   ____ enjoyed it somewhat
___ did not enjoy it much   ____ did not enjoy it at all

What did you like about it? _____

_____

What did you not like about it? _____

_____

Other comments: _____

_____

_____

Concert Report 2: Choral/Vocal Music

Choir/Chorus   ATTACH
Chamber choir/Madrigal choir   TICKET
Solo vocal recital   STUB
                                                                    HERE

Concert Setting

Date of concert: _____

Place of concert: _____

Name of group(s) performing: _____

_____

Describe briefly the group(s) performing (size, men vs. women):

_____

_____

Were concert programs provided? ___ yes ___ no. If yes, attach a copy.

Were program notes provided? ___ yes ___ no

Did the program include:

    the vocal texts that were sung? ___ yes ___ no

    translations of foreign language texts? ___ yes ___ no

Did the concert include instrumental accompaniment? ___ yes ___ no

If yes, check those applicable ____ orchestra ____ small instrumental group

____ harpsichord ____ piano ____ organ ____ other (specify) _____

Concert Music

Did the program include any of the following genres?

Choral		Solo vocal
___ Mass	___ oratorio	___ opera aria
___ part song	___ madrigal	___ Lieder
___ anthem	___ hymn	___ song cycle
___ motet	___ cantata	

List any other genres performed. _____

_____

Did you read about any of the works performed? ___ yes ___ no

If yes, where? ___ program notes ___ textbook ___ outside reading

What historical eras were represented on the program?

___ Medieval/Renaissance ___ Baroque ___ Classical

___Romantic ___ 20th century

Choose two works from the program. Name the composer, the work, and the movement (if applicable) and compare them in the following outline.

	FIRST WORK	SECOND WORK
Composer:	_____	_____
Title:	_____	_____
Movement or Section:	_____	_____
Melody:	_____	_____
	_____	_____
Rhythm/ Meter:	_____	_____
Harmony:	_____	_____
	_____	_____
Texture:	_____	_____
	_____	_____
Tempo:	_____	_____
	_____	_____
Dynamics:	_____	_____
	_____	_____
Vocal style:	_____	_____
	_____	_____
Mood:	_____	_____
Other:	_____	_____

What was your overall reaction to the concert?

___ enjoyed it a lot ____ enjoyed it somewhat

___ did not enjoy it much ____ did not enjoy it at all

What did you like about it? _____

_____

What did you not like about it? _____

_____

Other comments: _____

_____

Concert Report 3: Dramatic Music

Opera/Operetta   ATTACH
Musical   TICKET
Play with incidental music   STUB
                                        HERE

Concert Setting

Date of concert: _____ Location: _____

Composer/Author: _____

Title of work: _____

Were concert programs provided? ___ yes ___ no. If yes, attach a copy.

Were program notes provided? ___ yes ___ no

Did the program include:

     the vocal texts that were sung? ___ yes ___ no

     translations of foreign language texts? ___ yes ___ no

     a summary of the plot or action? ___ yes ___ no

Concert Music

In what language was the work performed? _____

In what language was it originally written? _____

Did you read about the work performed? ___ yes ___ no

If yes, where? ___ program notes ___ textbook ___ outside reading

Give a brief summary of the plot of this work.

_____

_____

_____

_____

Did the performance include instrumental accompaniment? ___ yes ___ no

If yes, was the music: ___ live or ___ prerecorded?

What instrumental forces were employed? If live, where were they placed?

_____

_____

Choose a selection from the work (an aria, a song, or an instrumental number), identify it in some way, and describe its musical features below.

Composer: _____

Selection: _____

Melody: _____

_____

Rhythm/meter: _____

_____

Harmony: _____

_____

Texture: _____

_____

Tempo: _____

_____

Dynamics: _____

_____

Vocal style: _____

_____

Instrumental style: _____

_____

Mood: _____

Other: _____

What was your overall reaction to the concert?
___ enjoyed it a lot   ____ enjoyed it somewhat
___ did not enjoy it much   ____ did not enjoy it at all

What did you like about it? _____

_____

What did you not like about it? _____

_____

Other comments: _____

_____

_____

Concert Report 4: Popular Music

Rock group   ATTACH
Solo singer or Instrumentalist   TICKET
Jazz combo or Ensemble   STUB
                                                        HERE

Concert Setting

Date of concert: _____

Place of concert: _____

Name of group(s): _____

_____

Did you know about the performer or group prior to this concert?
       ___ from recordings   ___ from MTV or radio
       ___ from a friend   ___ did not know

Concert Music

What was the makeup (instruments and voices) of the performance?

_____

_____

_____

How would you describe the style or genre of music performed?

_____

_____

Choose a selection from the concert that you can describe below.

Selection: _____

Melody: _____

_____

Rhythm/meter: _____

_____

Harmony: _____

_____

Texture: _____

_____

Tempo: _____

_____

Dynamics: _____

_____

Vocal style: _____

_____

Instrumental style: _____

_____

Mood: _____

Other: _____

What was your overall reaction to the concert?

___ enjoyed it a lot   ____ enjoyed it somewhat
___ did not enjoy it much   ____ did not enjoy it at all

What did you like about it? _____

_____

What did you not like about it? _____

_____

Other comments: _____

_____

_____

Concert Report 5: World Music

Concert Music

Date of concert: _____

Place of concert: _____

Name of group(s): _____

_____

Country(ies) or culture(s) represented in concert: _____

_____

Was there a concert program? ___ yes ___ no

Were there any: program notes? ___ yes ___ no

spoken remarks? ___ yes ___ no

Concert Music

What was the makeup (instruments and voices) of the performance?

_____

_____

_____

_____

What was unfamiliar to you about the music and its performance?

_____

_____

_____

What was familiar to you about it? _____

_____

_____

_____

Choose a selection from the concert that you can describe below.

Selection: _____

Melody: _____

_____

Rhythm/meter: _____

_____

Harmony: _____

_____

Texture: _____

_____

Tempo: _____

_____

Dynamics: _____

_____

Vocal style: _____

_____

Instrumental style: _____

_____

Mood: _____

Other: _____

What was your overall reaction to the concert?

____ enjoyed it a lot   ____ enjoyed it somewhat

____ did not enjoy it much   ____ did not enjoy it at all

What did you like about it? _____

_____

What did you not like about it? _____

_____

Other comments: _____

_____

_____

Post-Course Survey

Level:

___ Freshman ___ Sophomore ___ Junior ___ Senior ___ Grad

___ High School ___ Adult Education ___ Other _____

Major (or undeclared): _____

Minor area (or undeclared): _____

Have your musical preferences:

___ changed, ___ expanded, or ___ remained the same?

Which genres did you most enjoy studying in this course?

___ orchestral music ___ chamber music ___ opera ___ musical

___ choral music ___ ballet ___ solo vocal music ___ rock

___ jazz ___ traditional music ___ world music

Rate your general reaction to the music of the various style periods:

a. like very much
b. like somewhat

c. do not like very much
d. dislike

___ Middle Ages   ___ Renaissance   ___ Baroque

___ Classical   ___ Romantic   ___ 20th century

List two specific pieces that you enjoyed very much.

_____

_____

What is it about them appealed to you? _____

_____

List two pieces that you did not enjoy hearing.

_____

_____

What is it about them did not appeal to you? _____

_____

Musical Listening

During this course, did you:

___ attend concerts?   If so, how many? _____

___ watch TV broadcasts of concerts?   If so, how many? _____

___ watch videos of concerts?   If so, how many? _____

Do you enjoy attending concerts? ___ yes   ___ no

Will you now try new types of concerts? ___ yes   ___ no   ___

    maybe

Have you purchased any musical materials during the course (other than

course-required materials)? ___ yes ___ no

If yes, what have you purchased? _____

_____

_____

Course Assessment

What was most valuable about the course content? _____

_____

_____

What was most valuable about the textbook? _____

_____

_____

Was this study guide helpful to you in the course? ___ yes ___ no

Would you like to take another music course? ___ yes ___ no

If yes, what focus would you most enjoy?

    ___ classical music ___ world music ___ jazz ___ rock

    ___ music theory ___ performance ___ other _____

Other comments: _____

_____

_____